SALTBURN
PY.98

LUXURY
FLIGHT PETROLEUM Co Ltd
SERVICE
STATION
PARKHURST
GARAGE
OPEN DAY & NIGHT
Book here for
NO SMOKING
ALL LIGHTS
GLASGOW – LONDON
SIX
BRIGHTON
THREE
TRAVEL
ORANGE
JR 469
GN 9734

BRITISH BUSES OF THE 1930s

Alan Millar

 Patrick Stephens, Cambridge

First published 1982

British Library Cataloguing in Publication Data

Millar, Alan
British buses of the thirties.
1. Motor bus lines—Great Britain—History
I. Title
388.3'22'0941 HE5663.A6

ISBN 0-85059-496-0

Text photoset in 10 on 10 pt Baskerville by Manuset Limited, Baldock, Herts.
Printed in Great Britain, and bound, by The Garden City Press, Letchworth, Herts, for the publishers, Patrick Stephens Limited, Bar Hill, Cambridge, CB3 8EL, England.

Front endpaper *When United Auto took over the 11-vehicle Safeway Services fleet of J.B. Fraser of Redcar in 1931, this Thornycroft BC joined the combine company's fleet. The bus, which had a body built by W.G. Edmund of Middlesbrough, ran from Stockton to Middlesbrough, Redcar and Saltburn* (Michael Heard collection).

Frontispiece *A coincidental pair of Oranges. Orange Brothers, a Northumberland operator who ran from London to Newcastle and Glasgow, garaged their coaches at Flight Petroleum's premises in London's Holloway Road. Here, a 1933 AEC Regal with Weymann body stands to the left of an Orange Luxury Coaches Regal bound for Brighton. Orange Luxury was a completely separate business* (Robert Grieves collection).

Title page *A publicity leaflet for the Leyland Gnu six-wheeler launched in 1937* (Robert Grieves collection).

Rear endpaper *Southdown's publicity of the period included this model bus, complete with precocious child driver* (National Bus).

Back Cover Photographs

Left *A Dodge PLB operated by the North London-based City Coach Company. It provides a curious contrast for City's fleet of six-wheel Leylands* (D.W.K. Jones).

Right *A 31-seater Minerva which East Kent acquired with the Granville Coaches fleet at Margate* (D.W.K. Jones).

Below *A normal control Gilford 168SD with Duple 26-seat body which was new in 1930 to Skylark Motor Coach Company, of London. It was taken over by Green Line in 1932 and was photographed near its Poland Street terminus that year* (J.F. Higham).

CONTENTS

INTRODUCTION

Everyone has an image of the 1930s. Perhaps it is an Odeon cinema, *Picture Post*, sprawling suburbia or the *Queen Mary*. Maybe it is the Jarrow Crusade, Mosley's blackshirts, Ramsay MacDonald or Neville Chamberlain. It was a time of great change and drama and, for the bus industry in the British Isles, it was probably the golden decade when the endeavours of the preceding years bore fruit, and gave the industry a strong base from which to withstand the troubled years ahead. Little of the bus scene of the 1930s bore much resemblance to that of ten years earlier, yet much of the framework of the 1930s is still around 50 years later.

From being a business in which demobbed servicemen ran war surplus vehicles, the industry had grown up into a much more professional and better financed regime. And the development of pneumatic tyres and such low-framed chassis as the Leyland Titan of 1927 and the AEC Regent of 1929 had put the bus at least on a par with the tram and train. Legislation, such as that contained in the 1930 Road Traffic Act, imposed a rigid discipline upon the industry, but it was one from which it was to profit more than it was to suffer at the time; and a process of mergers of fleets into larger units, which had already begun, gathered momentum with the passage of the 1930 Act.

The high spots of flamboyant 1930s' design largely passed the bus by, but as an efficient piece of machinery, the bus of 1939 was a testimony to engineering progress. Maybe it did not look radically different, but it was a stronger, more reliable, longer lasting and more economical vehicle than anything which had gone before. This account of the period is a general one and does not pretend to detail every twist and turn of the decade. I have drawn upon case histories where they highlight trends or reveal important exceptions to a general rule, and I have chosen September, rather than December 1939 as the end of the decade. The last months of 1939 belong to a history of the 1940s.

The better motor coaches of the 1930s offered the style and comfort of contemporary luxury private cars. One of Black and White's 1937 Bristol JO6Gs with Eastern Coach Works 30-seat body prepares to leave for London (J.F. Higham).

AN IMPOSSIBLE STATE OF AFFAIRS

When transport minister Herbert Morrison described Britain's bus and coach licensing system in 1930 as 'an impossible state of affairs which must be cleared up', he wasn't just making a political point. It really was a tangled mess, with 1,298 local licensing authorities empowered by various pieces of Victorian legislation to issue hackney licences so that buses could ply for hire in their areas. Trams and trolleybuses were run by statutory authorities and were subject to the minister's control, but the motorbus and coach scene was a hotch-potch, with numerous complaints of inconsistent decisions being taken often by neighbouring authorities. There was also a widespread belief that far too many under-financed buses were chasing each other for a limited amount of traffic, and that public safety was being placed at risk by operators who failed to meet satisfactory maintenance standards and whose services ran to no fixed timetables.

The Labour Government's answer was to draft a Bill which became the 1930 Road Traffic Act, the first example of comprehensive legislation which took account of the motor bus. Strict conditions were laid down for a bus industry which, hitherto, had enjoyed wide freedom. Tough months followed as the industry grew accustomed to the new regime. A minimum age limit of 21 was introduced for bus drivers who also had to pass a test, and conductors, too, had to obtain a licence. And all buses and coaches with eight seats or more were restricted to 30 mph, actually 10 mph higher than the previous limit, but more strictly enforced.

From April 1931, regulations were introduced which banned crews from smoking, from speaking to each other without reasonable cause and from stopping buses at the roadside for unnecessary periods. Passengers, too, had to toe the line and were forbidden to distract the driver's attention or to indulge in such anti-social behaviour as using obscene language, smoking in prohibited areas, damaging the bus, playing noisy instruments, shouting or trailing balloons and streamers from windows. You could even be thrown off a bus for wearing offensive clothing. Every bus had to be covered by third party insurance, and to carry a public service vehicle licence, indicating the type of service on which it could be used. That was not issued unless the vehicle had a valid certificate of fitness issued by a certifying officer or a public service vehicle examiner. These were valid for up to five years, depending on the condition of the vehicle, and were only issued if the vehicle measured up to the Construction and Use Regulations.

From 1931, a four-wheel double-decker could not exceed 26 ft in length (excluding its starting handle), and the equivalent limit for single-deckers was 27 ft 6 in, while six-wheelers could be 30 ft. The width limit was 7 ft 6 in and there was a 15 ft overall height limit for double-deckers, 10 ft 6 in for single-deckers and a 9 ft 6 in limit between the ground and the lower saloon roof of a double-decker. All had to be tilted safely to 28 degrees, although vehicles registered before July 1 1931 needed only to be tilted to 27 degrees. The Act also had a controversial provision that a bus with more than 20 seats needed a conductor, unless no adult fare was less than 6d (2½p), in which case one-man buses could seat up to 26. This had a hard effect on operators who used small buses to open up services to new housing estates, and resulted in registrations of new 26-seaters dropping from 160 in May 1931 to only four in January 1932. Birmingham Corporation coped with this change by having 30 25-seat Guy Conquest bonneted buses converted in 1932 to 32-seat forward control single-deckers which made more economical two-man vehicles.

However, the most dramatic effect of the new Act came through the introduction of road service licensing. Now, an operator had to run to an agreed timetable with fixed fares and had to prove that demand existed for the service. Licences were issued for stage carriage services (where at least one fare was less than 1/- (5p)), express services, excursions and tours, and contract carriages. Private hires remained outside the scope of licensing. Existing operators were given priority over any new applicant for a service, existing services—especially trams and trolleybuses—were protected sometimes by placing limits on the number of vehicles used or the fares charged, and additional services were only permitted where there was a clear public need for them. These rules led to something of a last-minute panic as operators started sometimes unnecessary new services in order to stake their claim for consideration as established operators.

This mammoth adjudication was presided over by 13 Traffic Commissioners' chairmen, two in Scotland, the rest in England and Wales. Appointed by the transport minister, they headed traffic area offices, and each was assisted by two part-time assistants appointed by local authorities. Their starting salary in 1930 was between £1,000 and £1,200 a year, and the final selection from 2,000 applicants was made in time for them to take up duties on December 1 1930. Licence applications had to be lodged by January 1 1931, and the system swung into operation three months later. £1,000 might not sound like a large salary today, but senior examiners were only being offered around £300 a year, and psv examiners £260. A bus driver with one of the big companies might earn around £145 a year, compared with £182 for an average skilled worker at the time, and £109 for a labourer.

The very existence of legislation dissuaded many smaller firms from carrying on but, by May 1931, the 13 areas had received 32,000 licence applications, and had taken 3,249 decisions, including 154 to refuse licences. There also had been 27,000 applications for backing licences for services which started in one traffic area, and ran into others. Four months later, when around 40,000 applications had been received, the Commissioners reported that they had granted 86.5 per cent of applications, had refused 5.9 per cent, and the other 7.6 per cent had been withdrawn. The Commissioners' first public hearing took place on April 8 1931 when the East Midland Commissioners met to consider licence applications from Nottingham City Transport and West Bridgford Urban District Council. There were no objections and the hearing passed uneventfully. It was left to others to add colour.

From an early stage, it became clear that the main line railways would exercise their statutory right to oppose licence applications, and the Commissioners had to try to sort out fact from fiction in claims of buses sweeping traffic away from what turned out often to be inconveniently sited railway stations. This initial traffic court enthusiasm prompted the London, Midland and Scottish Railway to oppose a Walsall Corporation application for eight licences, saying that passengers would go by train if the buses did not exist. Walsall manager Vane Morland dismissed LMS' argument as 'motheaten', and railway objections to 36 services in neighbouring Wolverhampton were withdrawn rapidly.

Although licences tended to go to the major operators, there were some exceptions, such as when the Northern Traffic Commissioners prohibited Stockton Corporation from running to the village of Yarm and decided in favour of private operator Jones and Pritchard. Nor were the big boys above being told to toe the line. The Western Commissioners were quick to tell Plymouth Corporation to co-ordinate its services with those of Western National, rather than seek protective fares. There were occasions where long-established rural operators made it adbundantly clear that they would not be bound by a decision which went against them. And there was a memorable 16-hour hearing of the Yorkshire Commissioners in 1932 when L. Baddeley, of Huddersfield, called 12 witnesses to support an application for a service to Sheffield. The hearing ended at 2 am, but Baddeley lost the case. The astute operators were quick to learn the value of being legally represented before the Commissioners, and lawyers soon specialised in traffic court work. Among these was Edgar Lustgarten who was to gain post-war fame as a broadcaster.

Trade associations also developed to meet operators' needs, by providing legal advice to help with the preparation of licence applications. They helped smaller operators meet larger companies' competition, and assisted them in dealing with complaints from the public.

The Motor Hirers and Coach Services Association was based in London, and fought hard on its members' behalf, while an early provincial equivalent was the Northern Road Transport Owners' Association which was set up in 1930, in advance of the 1930 Act taking effect, under the chairmanship of leading north-eastern coachman Joseph Orange. Membership grew from an initial 12 bus and coach operators to 60 by January 1931, and that meant a combined 'fleet' of over 400 vehicles. In August 1931, the National Council of Public Service Vehicle Operators' Associations was formed, with representatives from the MHCSA, NRTOA and six other associations in the Midlands and South Wales.

Inevitably, there were many who were unhappy

with the Act's immediate effects, and they made much capital of anything which went wrong. There were reports of 'acute' inconvenience at the Whitsun bank holiday weekend in 1931, with some passengers being stranded at resorts because operators would have broken the law if they had put on extra coaches, and the railways could not cope. The MHCSA wanted Mr Morrison to lift all restrictions on coaches at weekends, but the law remained for 50 years. Strong words of protest came from Consett Urban District Council, in County Durham, which said services in its area had been cut, and it complained that, 'the requirements of the travelling public are not being met as a result of the actions of the Northern Traffic Commissioners'. Commissioners' chairman Henry Riches replied, saying much of the trouble lay at the feet of operators who did not pay high enough wages. It was not unknown for drivers to get only £2 for a 48-hour week. And he went on to kick the Council's complaint back into its court, saying:

'It is my experience that many members of local bodies do not care whether a bus service is running on a remunerative basis or not, so long as there is a bus waiting at their doorstep when they require it.

'It is natural that, in the execution of our duties, we are bound to annoy someone, otherwise we are not doing our job properly. I regard the annoyance of these people as a tribute to our work.'

John Pybus, who succeeded Herbert Morrison as Minister of Transport, did advise Commissioners to pay careful attention to the effects which their decisions might have on a small operator, and to help small operators bring out all the facts relevant to their case. In fact, the number of small operators declined steadily throughout the 1930s as the combine companies bought them out. By 1936, the total number of operators had dropped from 1931's 6,486 to 4,991, and that included a 6.73 per cent drop just between 1935 and 1936. The East Midland Commissioners noted a drop from 917 operators in 1931 to just over 700 in 1933 and, in September 1939, only 35 per cent of the independent operators providing stage services in Northumberland in April 1931 were still at work.

The reduction in the number of operators, and the swing away from smaller vehicles, weakened the less prepared manufacturers. While Leyland and AEC made great strides, TS Motors complained in autumn 1930 that they were not getting their usual business owing to customers' uncertainty about the Act's effects, and a year later Maudslay complained that bus orders had been 'seriously retarded by recent legislation'. Motor cycle builder A.J. Stevens, who built AJS single-deckers, went into liquidation in 1931, and Halley wound up their affairs in 1935. Many importers of small buses pulled out of the British market at the same time, although it is fair to remember that the world trade depression and associated import controls played their part, too. A staggering 45 per cent of the remaining market for 14-20 seat buses was captured by Bedford in 1932, its first full year on the market. Vauxhall launched the British-designed-and-built Bedford then to counter resistance to its Luton-assembled Chevrolets, and to gain export business, and stopped building the Chevrolet models early in 1932.

The Commissioners met early in their careers to smooth out inconsistencies in their work, and also to clear up some nonsenses which had been allowed to creep in. For instance, they soon stopped insisting on operators making personal appearances at hearings for backing licences, after a case in which a small proprietor made a 520-mile round trip to a hearing for which he waited five days before learning that no decision had been taken. The minister first heard appeals against Commissioners' decisions in 1931, but in 1933 Mr Pybus caused an uproar by revoking a London—Upminster licence held by Edward Hillman's Upminster Services Ltd. The minister claimed the service, which was used by 40,000 passengers a week, had been run illegally from its inception, but Mr Hillman, who gained Parliamentary support from Labour Party leader George Lansbury, successfully appealed against the move. The Court of Appeal ruled that Mr Pybus had exceeded his powers.

There were some South Wales operators who felt their Traffic Commissioners had exceeded their powers the same year when they interpreted the public interest as being the preservation of some miners' jobs. The Commissioners accepted Bedwas and Machen UDC's objection to an application by a Merthyr Tydfil operator to carry 200 miners daily from Dowlais to Bedwas Navigation Colliery, as there were 1,500 skilled unemployed miners in Bedwas, Trethomas and Machen, some of whom had been induced to move into the area 30 years before. The Commissioners' decision stood.

Initial experience with the Act convinced the Ministry of Transport that the borders of the Northern, Southern, South-eastern, East Midland, and Yorkshire areas should be altered slightly from mid-1932 to reduce the number of backing cases, and from January 1934, the Southern area disappeared into the South-eastern, Western, and East Midland areas. By then, the chairmen also were called Licensing Authorities and had been given goods vehicle responsibilities.

A complete free-for-all remained in the Irish Free State until May 1932, when the Road Transport

Act of that year required all operators of existing services to obtain road service licences from the Ministry of Industry and Commerce. Fares had to be agreed with the ministry, with the country being divided into two zones, one covering an area within a 15-mile radius of Dublin, the other for the rest of the Free State.

Much more far-reaching legislation followed in the 1933 Road Transport Act which raised the age limit for bus drivers from 17 to 21, introduced a bus driving test, controlled drivers' hours limits, made compulsory third party insurance, updated all traffic laws from 1861 onwards, and introduced speed limits of 20 mph for double-deckers and 35 mph for single-deckers. All buses with 14 or more seats needed a conductor and, from 1935, all four-wheel double-deckers had to comply with the British 26 ft length and 15 ft height limits.

However, of greater moment, the railway, tramway and canal companies were vested with compulsory purchase powers over independent companies, on the basis of ten years' purchase of the annual profit. The result was that, by 1935, private enterprise buses had all but vanished from Ireland's roads. Great Southern Railways took over the Irish Omnibus Company, which already ran services upon their behalf, along with several other operators, to gain a virtual monopoly of services outside Dublin, and the Great Northern Railway indulged in similar measures north of Dublin, including the takeover of all Free State services operated by Belfast-based H.M.S. Catherwood which also ran to Cork. The Londonderry and Lough Swilly Railway gained a similar monopoly in North Donegal.

Dublin United Tramways, by then associated with Scottish Motor Traction, invested £448,428 in acquiring all regular bus services in the Dublin area by December 1934, and added the Wicklow Hills company in Easter 1936. In mid-1934, DUT and 19 surviving independents ran around 300 buses in addition to DUT's trams, yet half of the buses were considered to be superfluous once the takeovers were complete. Around 35 per cent of the 600 busmen employed by the smaller companies became redundant as a result of the DUT takeover. Public fears of the effects of a monopoly were realised when an 11-week strike crippled services in 1935. On the other hand, fears entertained by some of the displaced independents that their buses would be replaced by trams proved groundless. DUT had already recognised that its future lay with buses and, after putting its much-expanded bus network into order, it started to replace the tram system with Leyland Titan double-deckers from 1938.

Northern Ireland enjoyed a system of limited competition until 1935, and indeed a route licensing system in Belfast had been used as a base from which Britain's Road Traffic Act was developed. But the 1935 Road and Railway Transport Act transferred most buses and lorries in the province to the Northern Ireland Road Transport Board. Only Belfast Corporation, Lough Swilly's Derry-Donegal services, buses with up to six seats, and hotel courtesy coaches remained outside its scope.

The NIRTB held its first meeting in August 1935 and, from October 1, it took over the Belfast Omnibus Company's 147 buses, the LMS Railway (Northern Counties Committee) fleet of 130 buses, Tilling-controlled H.M.S. Catherwood's 76 buses, GNR's Ulster fleet of 58 buses, and the Belfast and County Down Railway's 14 buses. After a year, it had taken over 61 operators and 692 vehicles of 27 different types, and streamlined this down to a summer peak of 475 buses by October 1937. This overnight nationalisation of prosperous bus companies by an uncomprisingly Unionist Government came as a bitter blow to operators like Catherwood, especially as it had also suffered a similar fate at the hands of the Free State administration, and many could see the Northern Ireland model being extended to Britain. In the province, there were suggestions that the NIRTB be merged with the Belfast undertaking and the railways, but moves in that direction did not start for another ten years.

Above right *Destination boards, already an archaic feature, grace the fronts of West Yorkshire Road Car Tilling Stevens single-deckers in Harrogate's Raglan Street in the early 1930s. A 1928 B10A2 is nearest the camera, with a 1927 B9 (rebodied in 1932) parked behind* (Michael Heard collection).

Right *The crew of a United Automobile 1929 Leyland Titan TD1 crank its starting handle before setting out from Newcastle Corporation's Haymarket bus station for Whitley Bay. Also in this 1936 view is one of Newcastle's Park Royal-bodied Daimler CH6 double-deckers and a Leyland Tiger owned by County Motor Services, of Choppington* (Michael Heard collection).

DUPLICATE CAR
HARROGATE
WW 7108

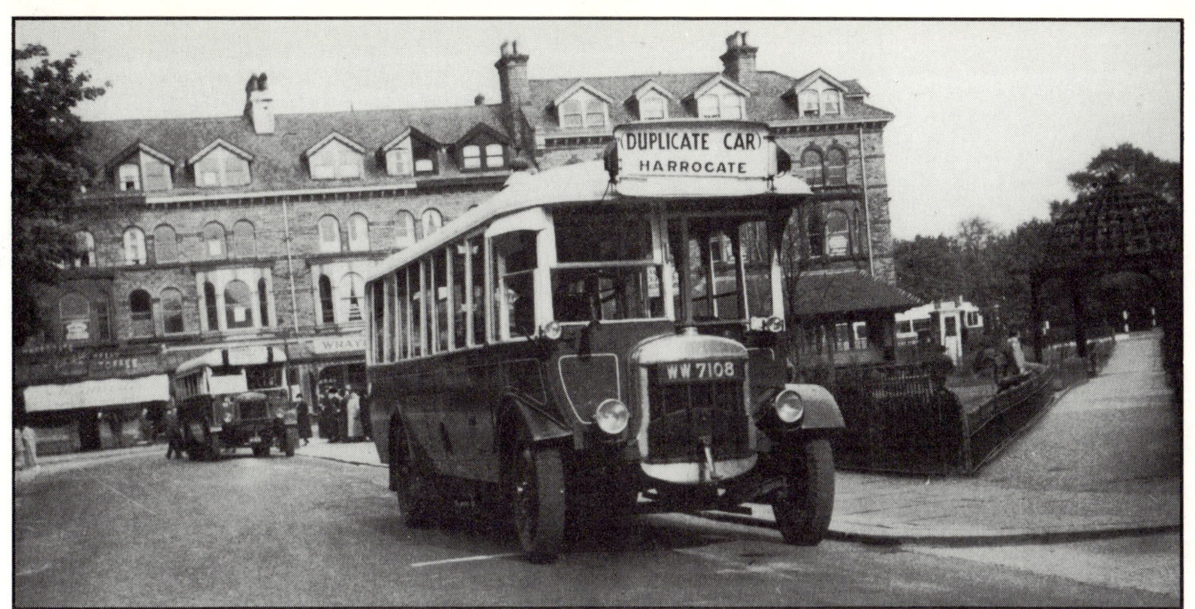

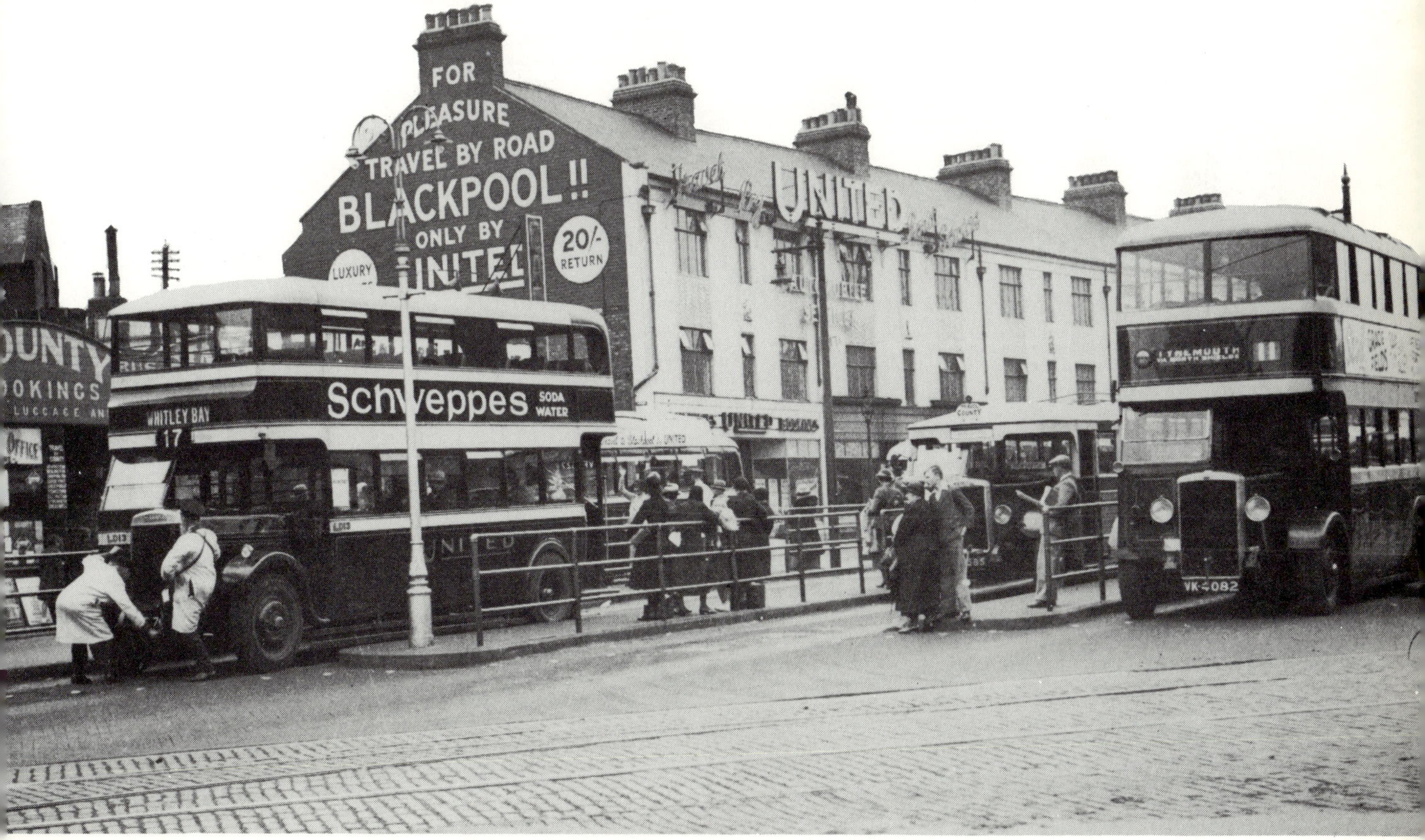
FOR
PLEASURE
TRAVEL BY ROAD
BLACKPOOL !!
ONLY BY
UNITED
20/-
RETURN
LUXURY
UNITED
Schweppes SODA WATER
WHITLEY BAY
17
VK 4082

Above *Typical of the small Bedfords which swept on to the British market is this 1937 WTB photographed in Bridge Street, Boroughbridge* (George F.T. Waugh collection).

Left *An AEC Regal operated by Western Welsh, one of the British Electric Traction companies* (J.F. Higham).

Below left *Bus stations were developed as the industry became more regulated. Derby's bus station, in which two of Trent's SOS single-deckers were photographed, was opened in October 1933 on the site of some of the city's worst slums* (D.W.K. Jones).

Above right *The epitome of the traditional village bus, this 14-seater Ford was operated by T.E. Jackson, of Thornton-le-Dale, in Yorkshire, on a service to Pickering* (Robert C. Davis).

Right *The petrol station, cars, wheelbarrow and fashions add period flavour to this view of a Northern Ireland Road Transport Board Dennis Lancet at the Dall Bridge, Cushendall, in County Antrim* (George F.T. Waugh collection).

VN 2398

PRIVATE
EZ-1823
RAC

Above *Enterprise and Silver Dawn used this Bedford WTB on its Scunthorpe town service. The 26-seater was new in 1936 and was fitted with locally-built Layne bodywork* (Peter White collection).

Below *A 1928 SOS QL operated by Northern General loading at Bishop Auckland. The double-decker is a 1932 AEC Regent in the Sunderland District fleet* (George F.T. Waugh collection).

Right *Construction and Use regulations eliminated such eccentricities as Glasgow Corporation's upper deck front emergency doors and escape ladders. F.D. Cowieson, who built the 60-seat body on this Leyland Titanic TT1, patented the feature. This bus, in fact, was never operated in Glasgow, but joined the Sheffield fleet* (Leyland Vehicles).

Below left *Manchester Corporation adopted a distinctive, streamlined appearance for its buses in the 1930s. This Leyland Titan TD4 with 52-seat body built jointly by Metro-Cammell and Crossley was new in 1937, and was photographed during the Second World War when it had been fitted with masked headlamps and white tipped front wings to cope with the blackout* (Greater Manchester Transport Museum Society).

Below right *British tilt-testing requirements also applied in Northern Ireland. Here, a 1938 Cowieson-bodied AEC Regent for the Northern Ireland Road Transport Board is subjected to the ordeal* (B.B. Boyle collection).

The 1930 Act introduced excursions and tours licences. Here is one of London-based Glenton Tours' all-weather Dennis Lancet coaches on an extended tour to Wales (J.F. Higham).

Alexander operated this 1933 petrol-engined Albion Venturer M81 with Northern Counties body. Albion lent the bus to the operator for the first few months of its life (Robert Grieves collection).

Typical of the small buses which swarmed the roads before the 1930 Act took effect was this Reo owned by Goads of Tenterden, in Kent (D.W.K. Jones).

Potteries Motor Traction bought 35 of the first Leyland Tiger TS7s in 1935. Like the others, this had a Brush body (J.F. Higham).

A Leyland Titan TD1 introduced to the Irish Omnibus Company's Cork city fleet in 1931. The piano front profile of the Leyland body was a distinctive feature of the Titan from its introduction in 1927 (Cyril McIntyre collection).

Trolleybus systems were operated under the terms of private Acts of Parliament. Southend-on-Sea bought four of these AEC 661Ts with English Electric bodywork and electrical equipment in 1932 and 1933 (J.F. Higham).

GETTING ON THE RIGHT RAILS

The story of the company-owned bus in the 1930s is linked inextricably with the main line railway companies which, under the Railways (Road Transport) Act of 1928, gained powers to run bus services anywhere in Britain, except London. Already, the Great Western, London, Midland and Scottish, and London and North Eastern Railways ran significant fleets of buses on routes which fed rail services, and there were real fears among existing operators that the new powers would encourage the railways to flood the roads with new buses, force them out of business, and then gain a monopoly of inland transport. Certainly, the railways' ambitions were unambiguous, as Southern Railway chairman Sir Herbert Walker made clear when he said: 'We aim to obtain control of all forms of transport in this country, and we shall not rest until we get it.'

However, the railways were run by astute businessmen, not megalomaniacs, as some wanted to believe, and they certainly had no wish to bankrupt themselves in a mad show of strength which would have pushed up everyone's operating costs and would have been of little, if any, benefit to the public. Instead, they bought shares in the larger companies which had emerged from the formative years of the 1920s, and by 1935 owned 15,000 buses in Britain.

In England and Wales, these were the companies of three groups, Thomas Tilling, British Electric Traction and Tilling and British Automobile Traction, the last being 32.9 per cent Tilling and 21.3 per cent BET, while the main Scottish group was Scottish Motor Traction.

By 1931, in addition to running its own fleets in London and Brighton, Tilling owned Hants and Dorset, West Yorkshire, Eastern Counties, Western National, Southern National, Eastern National, the National Omnibus and Transport Company (including Bristol Tramways and Carriage Company), and United Counties, of which all but the last two were railway financed. Of these, the Eastern Counties Omnibus Company was formed on July 14 1931 with £700,000 capital, and took over the Eastern Counties Road Car Company, the East Anglian wing of United Automobile Services, Peterborough Electric Traction, and the Cambridge-based Ortona Motor Company. BET's empire at the time comprised Hebble, Yorkshire Woollen District, Northern General, Midland Red, Devon General, City of Oxford, Western Welsh, Rhondda Tramways, South Wales Transport, Potteries Electric Traction (renamed Potteries Motor Traction in 1933), and Scottish General Transport. All but the last four were financed by territorial railway companies.

Tilling and BAT, which lasted from 1928 to 1942, took in Wilts and Dorset, Aldershot and District, East Kent, Southdown, Southern Vectis, Western Transport, North Western, Thames Valley, United Auto, East Yorkshire, Yorkshire Traction, Trent Motor Traction, East Midland, Lincolnshire Road Car, Ribble, Cumberland Motor Services, Crosville, and Caledonian Omnibus Company. Only Caledonian stayed outside railway control.

In Scotland, the LMS and LNER-owned SMT in turn owned W. Alexander and Sons who served the country's central belt and north-east. Late in 1931, they paid BET £1 million for Scottish General and Rothesay Tramways and, in June 1932, Western SMT was formed to acquire the group's interests in South-West Scotland. At the same time, Central SMT took over their interests in Lanarkshire and Dunbartonshire. LMS also had an interest in Inverness-based Highland Transport who, by 1939, ran 46 buses, and in David MacBrayne, who operated buses, lorries, and ships between Glasgow and the North-West of Scotland.

The railways also gained shares in bus services run by Yorkshire municipal undertakings, starting in Halifax and Sheffield. A joint committee of corporation and railways followed in Huddersfield in 1930, and the following year saw LMS paying £31,250 for a half-share in the Todmorden undertaking. Moves by the same railway to buy Lytham St Annes' bus and tram fleet at the same time came to nothing.

The reason for the railways' interest in buying shares (usually 50 per cent) in the major bus companies was not hard to see. Buses, often penetrating areas served only by token and sometimes inconvenient rail services, were gaining traffic at the railways' expense. In the Manchester area alone, the LMS' receipts dropped by 27 per cent between 1924 and 1930 and, nationally, bus competition and the trade depression reduced railway passenger journeys by around six per cent a year between 1930 and 1932. The railways, while by no means insolvent, wanted to gain a share of the new business. However, they were not satisfied simply to sit back and draw in their new receipts. There was little point in the railways' own fleets remaining in existence, and very rapidly most of the buses were transferred to territorial bus companies. For instance, LNER buses operating around Durham passed to United Auto and Northern General on January 1 1930 and, six months later, the company's former Great North of Scotland Railway services around Aberdeen passed to the SMT group.

By January 1 1934, when the Wyke Regis-Radipole service in Dorset passed to Southern National, the Great Western Railway's once 300-strong bus fleet had disappeared, mostly into associated companies' hands. Midland Red, Western Transport (merged in 1933 with Crosville), Bristol Tramways, City of Oxford, and Thames Valley took over GWR buses between 1930 and 1932. London General Country Services took over the Slough area buses in April 1932, as there was no railway-owned fleet in the area and, in any case, the London Passenger Transport Board was then only 15 months away.

Just as the railways' own fleets disappeared, so did many of their uneconomic rural rail services, and it was associated companies' buses which carried most of their passengers. In the first nine months of 1930 alone, LNER closed 88 stations, LMS 60, GWR 24 and Southern four and, in March 1932, Minister of Transport John Pybus told Parliament that the previous three years had seen the four companies close six branch lines and withdraw passenger services on 76 routes. These closures affected all parts of the country, and included 26 stations in Yorkshire and Northumberland which lost LNER services at the end of the 1930 summer season, and the Slammanan and Morningside branches in the West Lothian/Lanarkshire coalfield which were losing LNER £10,000 a year. In the south, Hants and Dorset had extra goods space provided in buses which replaced Southern trains between Fareham and Lee-on-Solent in January 1931, and in 1937 Aberdeen lost its suburban rail service owing to competition from railway-owned Alexander buses. Similar events were occurring in Ireland with, for instance, the Great Southern Railways withdrawing their trains between Galway and Clifden and Cork and Macroom in 1935. Buses took their place, just as they did in Northern Ireland when, for instance in January 1933, the LMS Northern Counties Committee closed its Limavady-Dungiven branch.

By 1931, the links between bus and rail had been strengthened to include the inter-availability of tickets, so that, particularly for long journeys, passengers could go one way by bus, and return by train. There were other links, too, with the GWR offering bus passengers its 'luggage in advance' service for journeys between London and the West Country and linking its parcels service with City of Oxford's bus parcels deliveries. In the same year, the LNER and United Auto boasted Britain's first bus/rail interchange at Norwich Thorpe station. A roof was built over the station forecourt and a bus ticket office provided, and bus passengers had access to refreshment, waiting room and toilet facilities in the station. At the same time, LNER published a summer timetable with a bus symbol against 380 'bus contact stations' where associated bus services linked with its trains.

A more eccentric fruit of road/rail co-operation was the Karrier Ro-Railer, a 26-seat LMS bus designed to run on road and rail and so combine the economics of bus operation with the speed of rail. Unveiled in January 1931, it was a standard Karrier Chaser Six petrol-engined single-decker fitted additionally with flanged rail wheels, buffers, a towing hook and screw-eye coupling. Its Cravens body had central doors on either side, each high enough for railway use and a sliding floor to bridge the gap between the bus and a station platform. It could be switched from road to rail in under five minutes by one man, according to the LMS, which conducted private trials with it throughout 1931. Its revenue-earning career was brief, starting on April 23 1932 when it began a road service from the Welcombe Hotel to Stratford-upon-Avon, and continued on rails to Blisworth. It was withdrawn on July 2 the same year, and apart from a one-day trial the following summer between Ashby de la Zouch and Leicester, was never seen again in public service. But it was still intact in 1936, when Karrier demonstrated it at a technical exhibition in

Frankfurt. The trouble with the Ro-Railer, clever as it was, was that it was neither fish nor fowl. By 1933, the LMS had ordered six motor railcars which fitted better into railway practice, and the first of 38 streamlined diesel railcars went to the GWR the same year.

Buses bought by the major companies were certainly more conventional than the Ro-Railer, and they became increasingly standardised as the 1930s wore on. In particular, the BET companies specified single-deck bodywork to an outline specification of its central purchasing organisation, the British Electrical Federation. Tilling companies relied increasingly on chassis built by Bristol Tramways and bodies from the Lowestoft works of Eastern Counties (renamed Eastern Coach Works in 1937), while SMT took a proportion of its bodywork from Alexander. Leyland and AEC took the lion's share of chassis orders from BET and SMT companies. A notable exception to this pattern was Midland Red (the Birmingham and Midland Motor Omnibus Company), which built its own buses, as well as meeting some of the needs of associated companies Northern General, Trent, and Potteries. Its SOS (standing probably for 'Shire's Omnibus Specification' after chief engineer L.G. Wyndham Shire) range was distinctive, and progressive.

In common with many company operators, Midland Red found itself having to graduate from single to double-deckers in the 1930s and, in 1931, it built the first of a large fleet of rear and forward-entrance 'deckers. Whatever technical attributes these double-deckers possessed, they were not a welcome innovation for company traffic manager Cecil Power who complained in 1932 that 'ill conceived' regulations which limited the number of standing passengers on single-deckers were forcing operators to use double-deckers on 'hundreds of routes' just to meet peak period loads. Despite such handicaps, the companies returned consistently good profits. Tilling and BAT, for instance, a £217,060 record for 1930, and five years later the figure was £328,718. SMT's 1930/31 profit of £135,244 had risen to a record £378,880 in 1938/39. As well as taking over many smaller operators' services, the larger companies were also able to carry many unprofitable routes on the backs of the money spinners, and in 1937 Southdown claimed that 63 out of 94 services did not pay their way.

The big companies also were better able to pay competitive wages to their employees, and the progress at SMT was typical of the pattern throughout Britain. From 1931, when a driver could earn 1/2½d (6p) an hour for a 48-hour week, this passed through a period of national wage cuts in 1933 until, in 1939, he could earn 1/5d (7p) an hour.

However, large companies could also be victims of their own size, as became apparent in 1935, when several major ones were hit by strikes in pursuit of increased wages. Only two years earlier, when unemployment stood at 2.7 million and the depression was at its peak, United Auto had been able to dismiss 25 per cent of its County Durham workers when they went on strike and replace them with unemployed drivers and conductors. Most crews at the time were male and, in 1938, Central SMT made it clear that it wanted to replace all its conductresses with boys who could later be retrained as drivers. While it found that girls were 'entirely satisfactory' on 29-32 seat single-deckers, it claimed they were less able to cope with heavy loads. On the other hand, August 1939 found war looming and Ribble were looking for conductresses as over 1,600 of their conductors were of presumed military age.

Some company buses remained out of combine control, either because their owners would not sell out or because the combines saw no value in becoming involved. One of the largest such groups was Red and White, based at Chepstow in Monmouthshire and serving South-East Wales, its home county, Gloucestershire and Herefordshire. In 1939, it amalgamated 11 subsidiary companies in the Swansea area to form the 130-vehicle United Welsh fleet, and the same year it bought Cheltenham District Traction from the Balfour Beatty group. By 1937, Balfour Beatty, through the Midland Counties Electric Supply Company, owned Mansfield District, Midland General and Notts and Derby, the latter having one of five company-owned trolleybus systems run in Britain in the 1930s. The other four were at Llanelly, Hastings, Mexborough and Swinton, and South Lancashire. Other proud outposts of independence were Provincial, with fleets at Gosport and Fareham and Grimsby, Barton in Nottinghamshire, and Lancashire United in the Greater Manchester area. None owed allegiance to a railway, but each was confined to a territory in much the same way as the combine companies had their spheres of influence.

Top *One of Alexander's 1937 Leyland Tiger TS7s climbs out of Low Street, Banff, en route for Aberdeen* (George F.T. Waugh collection).

Above *A pair of Waveney-bodied Dennis Lancet Is operated by York Pullman, an independent company which still survives. They were new in 1932/33* (R.C. Davis collection).

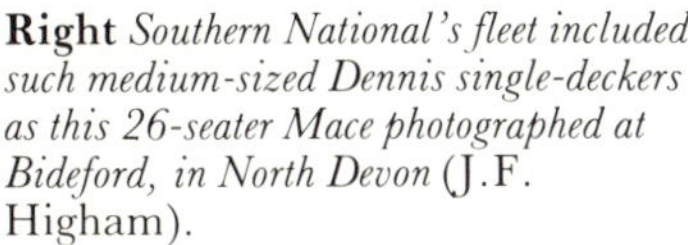

Right *Southern National's fleet included such medium-sized Dennis single-deckers as this 26-seater Mace photographed at Bideford, in North Devon* (J.F. Higham).

Above *Northern General's first 26 ft double-decker was this 1932 AEC Regent with 60-seat Brush body. The company bought relatively few double-deckers at the time* (Chris Warn collection).

Left *The Tilling and BAT-owned Wilts and Dorset fleet bought a large fleet of Leyland Titan TD1s, including this 48-seater lowbridge model delivered in June 1931* (J.F. Higham).

Above *Tilling and BAT formed Southern Vectis in 1932 to take over Dodson Brothers' Isle of Wight services. This Bristol K was photographed at Ryde Esplanade* (J.F. Higham).

Right *Although the Great Western Railway's last bus service from Radipole to Wyke Regis was taken over by Southern National in 1934, the GWR and Southern Railway names were carried by buses used on the service. This is a 1937 Bristol with Beadle bodywork* (D.W.K. Jones).

Above *Railway ownership of part of the Sheffield fleet is betrayed by the LNER lettering on the side of a 1936 Craven-bodied Leyland Tiger TS7c on the long Sheffield—Gainsborough route* (J.F. Higham).

Left *A busy scene in Scarborough's Vine Street bus station, with three 1935 Dennis Lancets and a 1937 Bristol J, all in the West Yorkshire fleet, and a 1937 Leyland Tiger TS7 in the East Yorkshire fleet* (G.H.F. Atkins).

Below left *A 1930 AEC Reliance ordered by the LNER, but delivered to United Automobile, stands in Newcastle towards the end of its 17-year life* (Robert C. Davis).

Above *The East Yorkshire Motor Services fleet included this 1935 Leyland Tiger TS7 with 30-seat Brush service bus bodywork* (J.F. Higham).

Right *A magnificent Maidstone and District Leyland Tiger with central entrance Harrington bodywork* (D.W.K. Jones).

Below right *A 1929 TSM B10A, rebodied by Eastern Counties in 1935, in service with North Western, a Tilling and BAT company* (J.F. Higham).

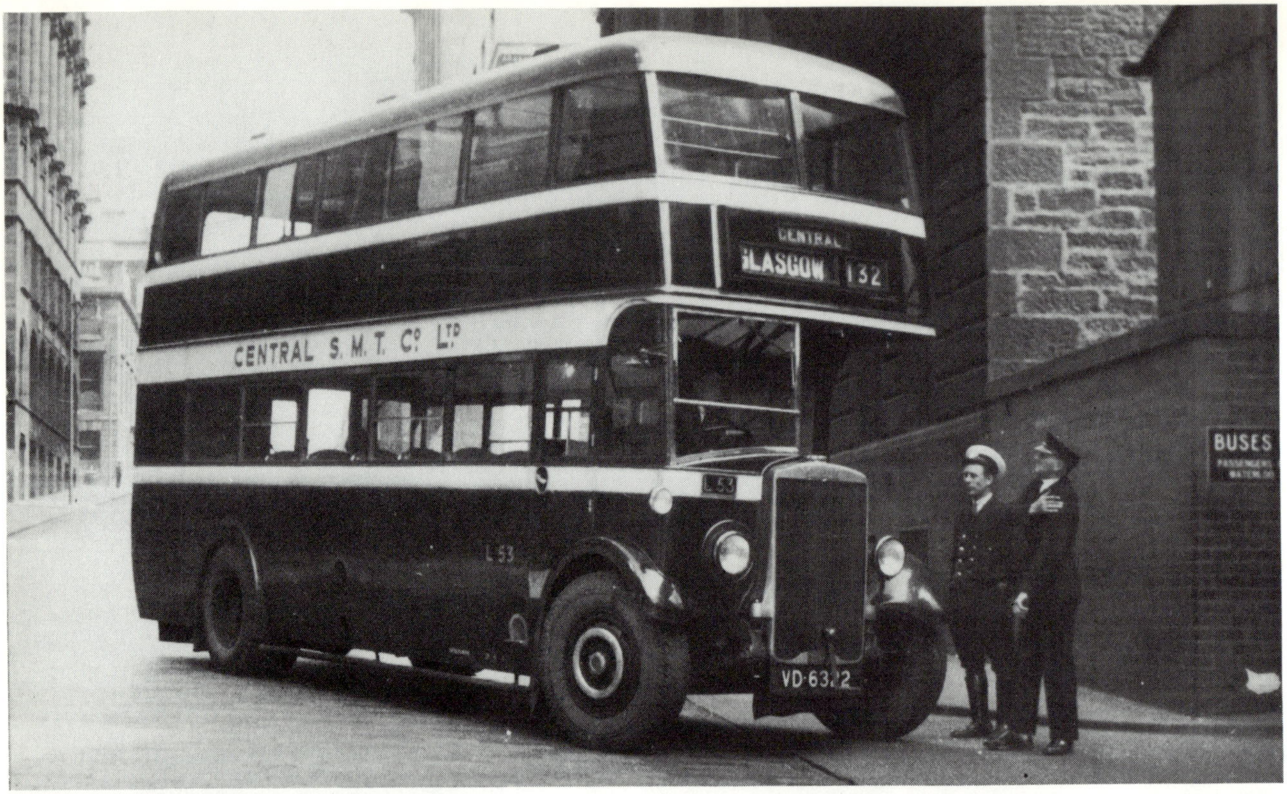
CENTRAL
GLASGOW 132
CENTRAL S. M. T. Co. Ltd
L53
BUSES

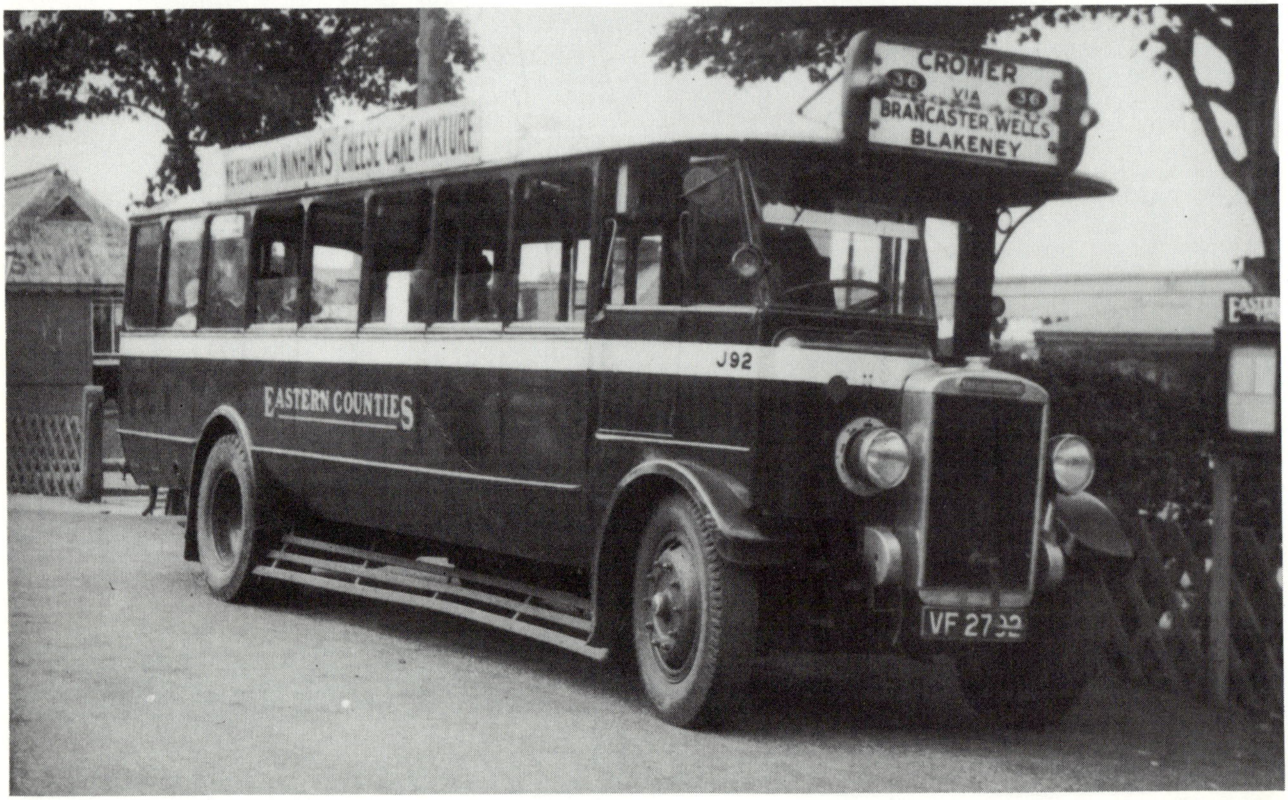
CROMER
36 VIA 36
BRANCASTER. WELLS
BLAKENEY
CHEESE CAKE MIXTURE
J92
EASTERN COUNTIES

Above left *Central SMT's Dunbartonshire and Lanarkshire sections met in Glasgow. Here, a 1936 Leyland Titan TD4 with 53-seat Leyland lowbridge body, enters the city's Waterloo Street bus station on a Dunbartonshire route* (J.F.Higham).

Left *Among the former United Automobile vehicles which Eastern Counties acquired at its formation in July 1931 was this 1928 Associated Daimler 425 with 35-seat United body* (J.F. Higham).

Above *A pair of highbridge Leyland Titan TD1s for Jersey Motor Transport is delivered on to a quayside in July 1932* (Leyland Vehicles).

Above right *The Bassett-Enterprise companies were absorbed by the Red and White group and helped form its United Welsh subsidiary from 1939. This is an AEC Regent* (J.F. Higham).

Right *Cumberland Motor Services' fleet included this AEC Regal photographed in Cockermouth* (Robert C. Davis).

Left *A 1939 Leyland Titan TD7 in the Lincolnshire Road Car fleet on the Skegness—Boston service* (Peter White collection).

Below left *Venture, of Basingstoke, bought this Park Royal-bodied AEC Regent in 1937. The company bought AECs and Leylands and opted for this particular vehicle by drawing lots after the two manufacturers submitted identical tenders* (J.F.Higham).

Below *Lawson, of Kirkintilloch, operated this Ford B with bodywork built in the same Dunbartonshire town by James Martin* (George F.T. Waugh collection).

OF DOUBTFUL MORALITY?

The motor coach has its own place in any history of the 1930s, not just in one such as this. It was as great a social leveller as the radio, cinema or paperback book, offering luxury travel to the masses at a price they could afford, and its contemporary styling, occasionally with touches of Art Deco, reflected that role. Little wonder that one commentator of the day christened the coach 'the people's land yacht'. It found fans in influential places. J.B. Priestley travelled by coach while researching his *English Journey*, which was published in 1934, and confessed to being astonished by the speed and comfort. 'I never wish to go any faster,' he claimed. 'And, as for comfort, I doubt if even the most expensive private motors—those gigantic, £3,000 machines—are as determinedly and ruthlessly comfortable as these new motor coaches. They are voluptuous, sybaritic, and of doubtful morality. This is how the ancient Persian monarchs would have travelled, had they known the trick of it.'

Writing in the *Daily Herald* in 1936, H.V. Morton credited the coach with reviving the talkative traveller. 'These coaches have brought back to the roads of England a heartiness that we rightly associate with the 18th and 19th centuries.'

Over-indulgence in superlatives? Maybe, but the industry was as aware of the revolution and, in 1930, Glasgow travel agent A.J. Thomson commented: 'People have got it into their heads that they must get to their destination by road. They seem to have a mania for road travel.' That mania really started in 1925, when Greyhound Motors started a daily coach service between Bristol and London and, by 1930, business was brisk and expanding, with London an inevitable magnet for operators. With a population of over eight million, Greater London was a good market in itself, and the comparative wealth of the capital created a demand for cheap travel between London and the depressed North of England, Scotland and South Wales. In 1931, coaches on all grades of work (including tours) were reckoned to have carried 32.8 million passengers, at 3/- (15p) per head.

Some idea of the scale of business for long-distance coach services can be gained from the experience of one Newcastle-upon-Tyne booking agent, Messrs Coxon, who was handling bookings for day and night services to London, Nottingham, and Glasgow, and for two-hourly services to Liverpool and Manchester, as well as less frequent services to other parts of England and Scotland.

The Merseyside Touring Co Ltd provided further competition on the Liverpool—London route in April 1930 when Jarrow Labour MP Ellen Wilkinson inaugurated its daily service with a 15/- (75p) single or 27/6d (£1.37½p) return fare. The journey by 26-seat Tilling Stevens took 10 hours 15 minutes.

Typical of the services run between Scotland and London was National Coachways' route from Glasgow via Edinburgh and Newcastle which started in 1930. Daimler CF6s with 26-seat Hoyal observation coach bodies incorporating large luggage areas were used on the journey, which started at noon and ended 19 hours later. The fare was 30/- (£1.50) single, or £2-10-0d (£2.50) return.

Golden West Line offered London—Bournemouth for 10/- (50p) single, 12/6d (62½p) day return, or 15/- (75p) period return, fares which Greyhound—running a service on behalf of the Southern Railway—was obliged to match with a new service run from November 1930 until June 1931. Midland Red started a Leicester—London run in May 1930 for 9/- (45p) single, or 14/- (70p) return.

Often, operators competed on level of service. Black and White Motorways bought a batch of 24-seat Leylands in 1930, for night runs from Cardiff and Cheltenham, and had their London Lorries bodies fitted out with Elsan toilets and 25-gallon roof tanks. Passengers were issued with magazines to while away their hours aboard. Cestrian Service had a Maudslay double-deck coach on its Sunderland—London service in 1930, and claimed that passengers enjoyed a better view as well as the absence of engine fumes and heat. Merseyside Touring ran a luggage van on busy weekends at no extra charge. Mind you, some fell victim to the cut and thrust business practices and, in 1932, the creditors of Main Lines Ltd, of Plymouth, learned of the unbridgeable gap between its £1,154 assets and £35,524 liabilities. It ran between London and Plymouth and Ilfracombe.

J.B. Priestley was surprised by the extent of Southampton's bus station in 1933, with its waiting rooms, booking office, refreshment bar and newspaper kiosk. 'All this was new to me. I had never realised before how highly organised this road travel is, with its inspectors and inquiry offices and waiting rooms and what not.' Coach stations, were a London phenomenon to begin with, and they stemmed from a need to improve upon roadside pick-up points outside booking offices. London Coastal Coaches (formed by combine companies to handle bookings) opened its Lupus Street station in Pimlico in April 1928, and by 1930 it boasted over 20 regular users and 300 coaches a day, with up to 900 on holidays. The London Terminal Coach Station in Clapham Road, opened in 1929 by Blue Belle Motors (taken over by Red and White in 1937), was used by independents and handled 11,000 coaches in 1931. Premises at King's Cross were part opened by Christmas 1931, but the daddy of them all, Victoria Coach Station was opened on March 10 1932 by John Pybus, who remarked that London Coastal had 'added dignity to the great industry of road transport by building so fine a station'. Built on a 1.5-acre site for £0.3 million, it was designed to hold 70 coaches, and handle 9 million passengers a year. Lupus Street closed, and a year later Victoria boasted 40 regular users, and one day in the summer of 1932, it handled 55,000 passengers in over 2,000 coaches.

Bournemouth Motor Stations Ltd opened a 50-vehicle terminus in the town in 1930, using a converted private house but, in May 1932, it was eclipsed somewhat when Hants and Dorset and Elliott Brothers (Bournemouth) Ltd opened a £100,000 combined bus and coach station to replace a terminus elsewhere in the town. Elliott's Royal Blue coaches, which ran between London and the West Country, used the bottom half of the station which had a white facade and neon lighting, and a sprinkler system as a protection against fire. Ironically, it was gutted by fire in 1976. Black and White Motorways, which was owned jointly by Midland Red, Bristol Tramways and City of Oxford, bought a large Georgian house at St Margaret's, Cheltenham, in 1931, and converted the 3.5-acre grounds into a parking area, part of which was glassed over. The house was adapted for its new role by installing central heating, a café and buffet, as well as a drivers' rest room and, as the decade continued, the station was to become one of Britain's most important.

The 1930 Road Traffic Act altered the rate of progress, and from January 1931 the rigidly enforced 30 mph speed limit meant that schedules had to change. Orange Brothers reported that the speed limit meant only an extra 25 minutes on its London—Newcastle service. It cut its breaks en route with, for instance, the stop at Doncaster reduced from 80 to 30 minutes. Generally, operators could be more honest when they published timetables than when they violated the old 20 mph limit, but did not admit to it.

There were a few short-lived attempts to get around the Act by using seven-seat limousines which were not covered by the legislation. Joshua Tulip of South Shields ran Buick saloons between Newcastle and London from December 1930, with a nine-hour journey, compared with 12 hours by coach. The fare was 22/6d (£1.12½p) single. Two months later, A.J. Thomson started a Glasgow—Southampton service via Newcastle and London, using six-seaters. The Glasgow—London fare was £2 single, and £2-8-0d (£2.40) to Southampton.

However, the most striking effect of the Act was the elimination of surplus capacity, as established operators gained licences in preference to newcomers, and the railways exercised their statutory right to oppose applications. The railways succeeded in getting the Traffic Commissioners to limit the number of duplicate coaches used on many services, and as hearings continued throughout 1931 they tried to have coaches banned from some bridges which were considered unsafe. The coach industry, inevitably, considered this a back-door move to stop competition. In fact, the coach operators had found a new market in most cases, rather than just poaching rail passengers, but the railways fought hard to get their share of the cheap travel market, and were offering such bargain fares as a 34/- (£1.70) overnight return from London to Newcastle in 1933, and evening returns of 4/- (20p) from London to Brighton and 2/- (10p) from London to Southend in 1934.

Such was the effect of rail competition, and the growth of use of small family cars, that 1932 was to remain a peak year for express coaches. That year, 19 million passengers were carried, and £3.4 million revenue was drawn in. In 1933, only 17 million passengers were carried, and revenue fell by more than 20 per cent to £2.7 million. Business bottomed out at 15 million passengers and £2.4 million revenue for the next two years, before climbing slowly to 18 million passengers and £2.5 million revenue in 1937, Coronation year. The golden days of the early 1930s may have been over, but the industry did become more efficient as the larger companies bought out the vast majority of independents and substituted higher-capacity coaches for smaller ones used before. On the other hand, the lack of competition between operators meant the loss of the little extras which had characterised the beginning of the decade. Liverpool coach operator C.F. Rymer complained in 1939 that coach travel was still in the 'cheap excursion class', whereas in 1930 every good class operator was experimenting with toilets.

The onward march of the big operator was relentless. The SMT group gained a monopoly of Scotland—London traffic in 1934, Crosville, which inherited Red and White's isolated Merseyside operations in 1934, had Liverpool—London to itself the following year, and United Auto was sole Newcastle—London operator from 1937.

Rather than risk losing all at a Traffic Commissioners' hearing, many firms saw virtue in pooling their resources on common routes, although these, too, became dominated increasingly by the larger partners. Yorkshire Services was the pool for operators linking the county with London, and the Limited Stop Pool covered the services between Tyneside and Merseyside. A Yorkshire-Blackpool pool, with Yorkshire Traction, West Yorkshire, Yorkshire Woollen, Hebble, Ribble and three independents, started in 1935 and saved 122,681 miles a year. The most spectacular pool was Associated Motorways, based on Cheltenham. Black and White, Red and White, Midland Red, and Greyhound started to co-ordinate services through the coach station from March 1934, and four months later, Associated Motorways started with Royal Blue and United Counties brought into the picture. Ribble also co-operated at a later stage. The result was a fantastic interchange of services from London, Wales, Devon, the North-West, Midlands and South coast several times each day which paid dividends for the partners. While they cut their mileage from 4.6 million in 1935 to 3.9 million in 1939, their traffic rose from 0.7 million to 0.9 million passengers.

Royal Blue became the brand name for all Western and Southern National coach services between London, Bournemouth and Devon from 1935, when the Bournemouth firm was bought from Elliott Brothers. From July that year, vehicle journeys were cut by 50 per cent, to give 13 departures each day from London via Bournemouth and another four via Salisbury. Feeder routes into Exeter were developed over the next four years.

Not only was London a focal point for long-distance coaches, but it also boasted a growing network of internal coach routes linking developing suburbs with the central area. Private operators, many with experience in the coastal or pleasure trade, had made such an impact that, by 1930, the London General Omnibus Company was complaining of having lost 8.5 million passengers paying 7d (3p) or more over the previous two years. General hit back on Easter Monday 1930 when the first of a large fleet of 27-seat AEC Regal coaches began a half-hourly Charing Cross—Windsor route in competition with Premier Line's Bush House—Windsor route which ran every 15 minutes. Both charged 2/- (10p) single, or 3/6d (17½p) return. However, that was only the beginning. The might of General was thrown into the creation of Green Line Coaches Ltd in July 1930 which, with the help of associate companies, had 275 coaches carrying 300,000 passengers a week on 27 routes by August 1931. Initially, the coaches terminated in central London but, to relieve traffic congestion, some cross-London working began in December 1930; and on Christmas Day that year a hastily erected coach station was opened in Poland Street, near Oxford Circus, on the site of a brewery which had only been cleared that August. To cope with heavy loads, a 50-seat AEC Renown double-deck coach was tried on the Redhill—Bushey route from September 1931, but found little favour.

Green Line lost some of its routes to longer-established operators when stage carriage licences were granted during 1931, but bought out ten of its competitors in 1932/33, and mopped up the rest under the compulsory purchase powers of the London Passenger Transport Board.

If the 1930 Act was a nuisance, a much stronger anti-coach lobby was a menace. Traffic congestion in London was getting worse, and the coach, as a recent addition to the roads, was an easy scapegoat, as was evident from a letter sent by a Colonel King to the daily Press in August 1930. He expressed 'great regret' at the plans for Poland Street station, and hoped coaches would be banned from the central area as they increased congestion, and the passengers and their luggage were 'an impediment to pedestrians'.

Minister of Transport Herbert Morrison warned he did not intend 'tamely to submit' to the growth in coach penetration of central London and, in December 1930, unveiled a plan to ban coaches from much of the West End and to restrict their movement in a wider area. That was more than the operators could tolerate, especially as many of them were convinced it was all a plot invented by railwaymen who were jealous of the coachmen's ability to run further into central London. They said it was unfair to single out coaches when all forms of road transport were contributing towards the problem, and the Motor Hirers and Coach Services Association warned menacingly: 'Motor coach operators are a law-abiding, peace-loving section of the industry, but their love of peace, and it may be dared to add, their observance of the law, will be only in measure to the fair treatment that is meted out to them.'

A concerted campaign, with MHCSA sandwich-board men parading in London, and vociferous protests being lodged by General, Gilford Motor Company (builder of many of the independents' coaches), and the booking agents, forced Morrison to drop the plan in March 1931. Instead, Metropolitan Traffic Commissioners' chairman Gleeson Robinson was told to restrict coach access to the central area. In fact, Morrison, who resigned in the political crisis of August 1931, had passed the buck to Robinson and, in November of that year, the Commissioners' chairman revived the plan. Coaches, he said, were an express service, and the last part of their journey was uneconomical and caused needless congestion. He wanted them to terminate outside the central area and transfer their passengers on to existing public transport.

Such was the volume of appeals against the reductions in coach services which followed Robinson's deliberations that a special committee of inquiry was set up, with Lord Amulree as chairman. Eventually, Amulree relaxed some of the restrictions, but Poland Street, which suffered from being badly sited anyway, had to be deserted, and Victoria became Green Line's focal point from October 1933. That cost Green Line 24 per cent of its traffic and plunged it into losses for the rest of the decade.

Excursions and tours remained buoyant throughout the 1930s, rising from carrying 15 million passengers and earning £1.6 million in 1932 to 19 million passengers and £2.2 million in Coronation year. Day, half-day and evening excursions were a regular recreation at a time when car ownership rose only from just over 1 million to under 2 million. There also was a thriving private hire and special events business on a scale unimaginable today, as sports meetings, military tattoos and works outings drew in crowds. In 1933, the Tidworth Tattoo attracted 130,600 visitors, of whom 63,382 came in 2,881 coaches. Only 15,759 went by train. On two days in August 1939, Ribble provided 180 coaches for the Littlewoods Pools annual Liverpool—Blackpool outing, carrying 5,500 passengers each day in an eight-mile procession.

While most people took their holidays in the British Isles, there was a market for European tours to be tapped by the astute operator. In 1930, the Daimler Hire Company, from 1931 a Tilling subsidiary, expanded its limousine business to include Daimlerways, a luxury tour venture with 11 tours of 7 to 55 days. Destinations were in France, Spain, Belgium, the Netherlands, Germany, Switzerland, Italy, Austria, Hungary and Czechoslovakia, and prices ranged from £19 single to Nice to £225 for a Grand European Tour. Daimlerways' seven bonneted Daimler CF6 coaches sat 15 passengers in uncompromising opulence, and catered for an exclusive clientele. There was a lavatory, rear buffet (for afternoon tea), each passenger had a folding glass-topped table and smoker's companion, and luggage went in suitcases provided by the company. By 1933, unfavourable exchange rates had forced the company to hire the vehicles for £8-8-0d (£8.40) per passenger per day.

The less well-heeled probably saw more in Wallace Arnold, the Leeds-based operator's tours to Germany, who started in 1934. In 1935, they ran two 9- and two 16-day tours, all incorporating Rhine cruises, and entered into an agreement with a Cologne company the following year which meant they no longer needed to ship their own coaches to Germany. Other operators, including Red and White and Cotter's of Glasgow, were in the same market, and even in 1939, when relations between Britain and Germany were plunging into an abyss, Wallace Arnold added two more continental tours, one to the Rhine, the other to the Riviera. Wallace Arnold was one of the few operators who really made the most of advertising, and in 1936 they had a publicity film on show at 26 cinemas within ten miles of Leeds. While other operators did advertise, many did it cheaply and without the flair and style of the railways. Indeed, such was the apathy among coachmen that the MHCSA was forced to abandon a Travel by Road campaign and National Road Passenger Transport Week in 1934 when only £100 of the £6,250 needed for the campaign was raised by its 6,000 members. On the other hand, few of the operators probably saw any need for such a campaign. The 1930s were good years for the humble coach.

Always Travel
BETWEEN LONDON AND THE NORTH
BY
Charlton's Blue Safety Coaches Ltd.

The Original Sunderland and South Shields—London Service
RENOWNED FOR RELIABILITY AND COMFORT

ALL COACHES HEATED
RUGS SUPPLIED
LATEST TYPE LUXURY COACHES

DEPARTURE TIME-TABLE.

King's Cross Motor Coach Station, King's Cross -	9.0 a.m.	9.0 p.m.
NEWCASTLE (Haymarket)	8- 0 a.m.	and p.m.
Hebburn (Garage) - - -	8-15 ,,	,,
South Shields (Mile End Rd.)	8-30 ,,	,,
Sunderland (Crowtree Rd.) -	9- 0 ,,	,,
Houghton-le-Spring (Church)	9-15 ,,	,,
Durham (Market Place) - -	9-25 ,,	,,
Darlington (Grange Rd.)	10-15 ,,	,,

RETURN TICKETS AVAILABLE
FOR 3 MONTHS
AIR-CUSHION SEATING

London Office:
10, Caledonian Road, N.1.
Phone: North 2544.

HEAD OFFICE:
Charlton's Blue Safety Coaches Ltd.
Red House Garage,
HEBBURN-ON-TYNE.
Phone 125.

Newcastle Office:
Haymarket Travel Bureau,
4, Haymarket.
Phone 22762.

Top *Simple early 1930s publicity for a Newcastle—London service begun in 1928. By 1937, United Auto had bought out all the competition on the Great North Road* (Chris Warn collection).

Above *A Gilford 168OT of Imperial Motor Services, of Liverpool, at the London Terminal coach station, in Clapham, in 1930. The fully-fronted body was built by Lewis and Crabtree* (J.F. Higham).

TEL. NO.
BRIGHOUSE 1

WOOD'S SUPER RADIO LUXURY COACHES

TEL. NO.
LOW MOOR 95

Tariffs and Particulars on Application

CHARLES WOOD LTD., 52 BRIGGATE, BRIGHOUSE AND TOWNGATE, WYKE

Top *Hardly a bare head in sight as a chocolate sales boy and newspaper salesman mingle with travellers preparing to board East Kent Tilling Stevens B49C2 coaches at London's Victoria Coach Station* (National Bus Company).

Above *A publicity postcard for a Yorkshire operator's coach fleet featured an AEC Regal. Valve set radios became a popular feature on coaches from the early 1930s* (Robert Grieves collection).

Right *The contemporary architecture of Victoria Coach Station has towered over London's Buckingham Palace Road since 1932* (National Bus Company).

Below *Black and White's St Margaret's coach station at Cheltenham was developed from the Georgian house to the left of this photograph. Here, B&W and Bristol Tramways Bristols load with passengers for Southsea and Weston-super-Mare* (J.F. Higham).

Bottom *A few operators tried using seven-seat limousines in an attempt to overcome the 1930 Road Traffic Act speed restrictions, but the other economies of large coach operation prevailed. This is a Hudson Super 8 used briefly on a Glasgow—London service* (Robert Grieves collection).

Above *Still bearing its former owner's name, a Thames Valley Gilford on a Reading—London service* (J.F. Higham).

Left *A Duple-bodied Leyland Tiger TS7 taken over by East Kent in 1937, along with the New Cross, South East London business of MT (Motor Coaches) Ltd and its London—Thanet services. The coach was one of five owned by MT, and was new in 1936* (D.W.K. Jones).

Below *A pair of Standerwick Leyland Tigers pose for the camera in 1937. The leading coach is a 1936 TS7 with Duple body, which started its career in the parent Ribble fleet* (Leyland Vehicles).

Above *Midland Red went against the trend in 1935 by building 25 bonneted SOS OLR coaches for its touring fleet. The red and yellow coaches offered saloon car standards, with canvas roofs fitted to their 29-seat Short Brothers bodies* (J.F. Higham).

Right *Alexander invested around £130,000 in 85 Coronation class coaches for their Bluebird fleet in 1937. The Leyland Tiger TS7s had steel-framed Alexander bodies. This one was photographed at the Arrochar Hotel, in Dunbartonshire* (George F.T. Waugh collection).

Below *One of Barton's Leyland Tiger TS7s on a tour* (Leyland Vehicles).

Top *And granny came too. A busy scene in August 1937 as a Green Line AEC Regal loads at Ecclestone Bridge, at Victoria, London* (London Transport).

Above *Lincolnshire Road Car had this 1933 Leyland Tiger coach fitted with a streamlined body by W. Rainforth and Sons of Lincoln. Wind tunnel experiments at the National Physical Laboratory suggested that it would save petrol but, given the 30 mph speed limit, a diesel engine would have caused less trouble* (J.F. Higham).

Top *Seaside crowds of this size were a common pre-war sight. The driver of a Southdown coach sorts luggage on the roofrack at Clacton's Lower West Promenade in May 1939* (George F.T. Waugh collection).

Above *A refreshment stop for a Leyland Tiger on a George Ewer service from London to Suffolk* (J.F. Higham).

493

AEC REGAL
32 SEATER DE LUXE COACH
A. MULLINER LTD
NORTHAMPTON

Top left *Observation coaches, with large luggage capacity, were run by a small number of operators. Blue Belle Coaches, a London operator taken over by the Red and White group in 1937, specified this layout for this 1937 Albion Valkyrie* (Alan Millar collection).

Above left *A mix of art deco style and Celtic aspirations on a streamlined Leyland Tiger in the Great Southern Railways fleet in the Irish Free State* (Cyril McIntyre collection).

Left *More wild styling, this time on an AEC Regal bodied by Arthur Mulliner, of Northampton* (George F.T. Waugh collection).

Top *Aerodynamic styling on a Foden coach for Whieldon's Green Bus fleet, of Rugeley, in Staffordshire. This view was used in contemporary Foden publicity material* (George F.T. Waugh collection).

Above *Varsity Express, which ran from Cambridge and Oxford to London, was taken over by United Counties in 1933. This AEC Regal was photographed on the Oxford service which ran outside United Counties' operating territory* (J.F. Higham).

Top *The Royal Blue name was adopted for all Western and Southern National long-distance services from 1935. This is a petrol-engined Bristol JJW delivered that year* (J.F. Higham).

Above *One of the Duple-bodied Leyland Tigers which Crosville ran on its Liverpool—London services. The company, which served Cheshire and North Wales, gained a monopoly of the Merseyside—London routes in 1935* (R.L. Wilson collection).

SOMETHING SPECIAL FOR LONDON

London's almost unstoppable growth, in the years before British governments tried to direct industries into the less prosperous provinces, was a pressing problem for transport operators. The population of the 1,846 square mile area in a 25-mile radius of Charing Cross had shot up from 8.3 million to 9.2 million between 1921 and 1931, and was to grow to 9.9 million by 1939. Something special had to be done to cater for the needs of such a fast-developing community. That something special was the London Passenger Transport Board, a public monopoly board modelled on the Port of London Authority, Metropolitan Water Board, Central Electricity Board and the British Broadcasting Corporation. Its architect was Herbert Morrison and, in many ways, it was a prototype for the nationalised industries created after the election of the next Labour Government in 1945.

Morrison's London Passenger Transport Bill was published in March 1931, and called for a Board run on business lines, free from as much political interference as possible and managed by board members who would look freshly at the whole of London's transport, without displaying any tram, tube railway, or bus bias. On the other hand, they were to be given powers to abandon trams. Morrison's aim in giving the board a monopoly of all public transport (except main-line railways) in the 1,846-square mile London Transport Area was to eliminate waste. At the Bill's second reading, he told the House of Commons that if competition involved a needless charge of even ¼d (0.1p) per passenger journey, this would still cost £4 million a year. That money, he contended, would be better spent on service improvements and reduced fares.

While there was competition on London's bus routes, by provincial standards it was hardly wasteful. The Metropolitan Police regulated routes and timetables, and operators competed on fares, comfort and standard of service. Safety standards were rigid, possibly to a degree of obsession which sometimes stifled innovation, such as when the first Green Line double-decker had to run without a platform door to meet police requirements.

The capital's largest operator was the London General Omnibus Company, part of the Underground Electric Railways combine, with a fleet of over 4,000 buses. Thomas Tilling had over 300 buses on London routes and, by 1933, there were still 56 independents in the Metropolitan Police area, with an average fleet of five buses.

E.G. Hope's Pembroke service was typical of the surviving independents. With only one bus, a Birch-bodied AEC Regent 56-seater, he was running between Camden Town and Coulsdon on weekdays, and between Oxford Circus and Southall on Sundays. Regular passengers were assured of the same seats each morning and the bus ran effectively to a limited stop schedule.

The 1,300 square miles which were to form the Board's country area were less strictly regulated, but again were dominated by the Underground combine, from January 1932 under the control of London General Country Services.

Morrison's Bill appealed to the combine and its chairman, Lord Ashfield, who had little to lose and probably plenty to gain from their new-found monopoly; but the independent operators viewed it very differently. Association of London Omnibus Proprietors chairman Arthur Partridge, whose Chocolate Express company ran six Leyland double-deckers mostly on the 11 route between Liverpool Street and Hammersmith, complained that the Bill was 'nationalisation pure and simple'. He said a growing London needed a transport service which could grow with it, and pleading to the nation's love of the underdog said: 'The public highway is free to peer and peasant, and should remain so'.

Commercial Motor considered the Board 'an unwise and dangerous experiment', and added: 'It is to be governed by a board of super men—a type always difficult to find, and still more difficult to replace'. That board of super men, hardly surprisingly, was chaired by Ashfield, and UER managing director Frank Pick was vice-chairman and chief executive officer. With them were five part-time members, Transport and General Workers Union assistant general secretary John Cliff, Hudson's Bay Company governor Patrick Ashley Cooper, London County Council alderman Sir John Gilbert, Surrey County Council alderman Sir Edward Holland and London and Home Counties Traffic Advisory Committee chairman Sir Henry Maybury.

Ashfield and Pick made a formidable team. Ashfield was a born manager with impeccable contacts at the highest levels of business and politics. He saw himself in the same mould as Lord Beaverbrook, whom he succeeded as MP for Ashton-under-Lyne between 1916 and 1919, and held directorships of the Midland Bank and Imperial Chemical Industries. Pick, by comparison, was an introvert with a keen sense of detail and design. It was he who translated much of Ashfield's broad strategy into practice and his sense of design meant that the Board inherited the combine's already high standards of industrial design and publicity material. Pick commissioned an alphabet which first appeared on Underground publicity in 1916 and which is still in use throughout London Transport today. Posters used during the Pick era have become classics; and the same attention to taste and detail was lavished on buildings and vehicles built for the combine and Board at that time.

July 1 1933 was the big day when the Board began to operate, although it was May 1934 before the now familiar London Transport trading name started to be used. After six months' operation, the monopoly powers over local bus traffic became effective, and then operators needed written LPTB permission to carry local passengers in the area. But the Board was restricted, too, as it was forbidden from operating long distance coaches, excursions and tours, or private hires beyond ten miles of its area. Some of the companies which lost their bus services—notably the City Motor Omnibus Company—were to switch to areas from which the Board was excluded.

The first day found the Board's central area with 4,224 ex-General buses, 55 from the General-owned Overground fleet at Potters Bar and 33 from the British fleet of Tilling and BAT. The country area, run until 1939 from Reigate, started with 447 buses and 446 Green Line coaches. Takeovers of central area operators started on October 1 1933 when Tilling's 86 Tilling-Stevens and 283 AECs were acquired along with three garages, a repair depot and 2,352 employees. The independents' 277 buses, mainly Leyland and Dennis double-deckers, started to join the Board's fleet 29 days later and the process was complete on December 4 1934 when Ponders End-based Prince Omnibus Company ran for the last time. The country area became embroiled in frontier exchanges from the beginning, and on the first day some of the LGCS routes passed to such railway-owned companies as Maidstone and District and Southdown, while Maidstone and District, Thames Valley, Aldershot and District, and Eastern National all transferred part of their operations to the Board. By 1938, the country area had taken over 284 routes from 72 operators, some of whom had sold out initially to railway-owned companies.

While Tilling and the independents could not stop the Board from taking over their assets, they fought hard for the best compensation. Few had garage premises which the Board could use, and when initial negotiations broke down, it was left to the London Passenger Transport Arbitration Tribunal, set up in September 1933, to strike compromises. Tilling claimed over £3 million compensation, saying it had lost revenue, but still had overheads to support. The Board, which felt that the operators were being selfish, offered £1.03 million. The Tribunal accepted that Tilling had suffered, and made an award of £1.7 million with an £82,500 severance payment. The other operators claimed £2 million in total and, after nearly three years, the Tribunal paid out £2.3 million cash and £2.6 million stock in the Board to 65 undertakings. For example, Premier Omnibus Company (15 buses) claimed £340,000 and got £199,500; Renown Traction (nine buses) claimed £64,000 and got £29,772; and Ryan Omnibus Company (two buses) claimed £24,000 and got £8,204.

Just as it was inevitable that the Board would be dominated by Underground combine management, so it was inevitable that General's vehicle policy would dominate from 1933. The Associated Equipment Company (AEC), an Underground company, built most of the General's buses from before the First World War and General's Chiswick works provided the bodywork. The Board had powers to go on manufacturing at Chiswick, but AEC had to be sold. Attempts to sell the company to Leyland and Ford failed but it continued as London's principal bus builder, initially with a ten-year contract to fulfil 90 per cent of the Board's new bus requirements.

General entered the 1930s buying 49-seat AEC Regents (type ST) and 56- to 60-seat Renowns (type LT) for double-deck work, and Regals and Renowns for single-deck routes. The six-wheel

Renowns were 'almost the ideal vehicle', according to company chief engineer George Shave in 1931, but a year later the Regent was being supplied as the 60-seat STL class and the more complex six-wheelers fell from favour. The STL, in 56-seat form, became the standard double-decker for the Board throughout the 1930s, and variants were built to suit special needs, such as services through the Rotherhithe and Blackwall tunnels. Some for the country area had forward entrances.

Pick's patronage of good design started to have a dramatic effect on the bus fleet from the mid-1930s. A fully-fronted STL, numbered STF 1, appeared in 1935, but despite its sleek lines, it proved impractical and was rebuilt conventionally. But the following year, a Chiswick design team led by Eric Ottaway produced the first of 340 Regal and Renown coaches for Green Line and private hire work, all with balanced, modern lines which put most provincial designs into the shade. However, the pinnacle of their efforts was reached in 1938, with the completion of the first RT-type double-decker, a 9.6-litre Regent fitted with air-operated pre-selective gearbox and low bonnet line. After running incognito for two months with a secondhand open staircase body, it was fitted with an Ottaway-designed body, again of very advanced design, and re-entered service in July 1939. Another 150 followed, but not until after war was declared.

Although Tilling and some of the independents bought AECs, Leyland had the lion's share of business with the small operators, thanks largely to generous financial deals which they and London coachbuilder Christopher Dodson had offered. Over 200 ex-independent Leylands, mostly Titan TD1s and TD2s, joined the Board's fleet and helped establish the company as supplier of the other ten per cent of the vehicle requirement. For motorbuses, that meant a fleet of Leyland Cubs for lightly-loaded services, eight Cub observation coaches for Inter Station services started in 1936, and 100 special Titan TD4 double-deckers delivered in 1937 to replace the last of the 2,116 1920s NS-type double-deckers which the Board inherited from General. There also were some exciting technical developments between Leyland and the Board, as described in Chapter Seven.

Leyland's good fortune was not shared by Gilford, which was the independents' other big supplier. Their lightweight, but powerful coaches and single-deck buses had found favour with many independents from their launch in 1925 and, thanks to hire purchase deals similar to Leyland's, they had gained a respectable share of the London market. But they did not have the back-up of large customers which Leyland also enjoyed, and the absorption of 220 Gilfords into the Board's fleet, so soon after the provincial market had started to go Leyland, AEC, Bristol, and Bedford's way, took the ground away from under their feet. They went into liquidation at the end of 1935, with a net deficit of £116,082.

The central area services came under the jurisdiction of the Metropolitan Traffic Commissioners from July 1933 and, at their insistence, the Board started to introduce fixed bus stops on its routes from March 1935. The compulsory and request stop signs, still part of the London scene, were another product of Pick's design sense.

The priority in the country area was rationalisation, and the first two years of the Board's existence saw widespread changes as routes were thinned out and new and rebuilt garage facilities were provided to replace cramped and inadequate premises inherited from smaller operators. Inevitably, some passengers were unhappy, and Sir Arnold Wilson MP complained in 1935 that services which had provided income for independents were being dropped because the Board could not make them pay.

When the Board refused to grant licences to coach operators who wanted to run tours to the 1935 Silver Jubilee decorations, the Motor Hirers and Coach Services Association lodged the highest level of protest possible. It sent a telegram to King George V, claiming that 25,000 passengers were being prevented from seeing the decorations. The Board relented and granted a third of applications—up to 50 coaches—but no more, because it said street closures were affecting regular services. When buses were prevented from running at King George VI's coronation in 1937, it was for a very different reason. London's central area buses were crippled by a strike which became a milestone in the history of British labour relations.

The 27,000 central area busmen represented a very strong group within the Transport and General Workers Union, and its Rank and File Committee included Communist Party members who had helped keep wage rates above the national average. By 1936/37, when average scheduled speeds of buses had risen from 1927's 9.67 mph to 10.42 mph, the busmen claimed a reduction in their working day from eight and a half to seven hours. They modifed this later to seven and a half hours, but backed up their case with evidence of irregular hours, faster schedules and carbon monoxide fumes damaging drivers' health. Negotiations did not get very far and central area buses stayed in their garages from May 1 to 28. Attempts to spread the strike throughout London Transport failed, and it ended after TGWU general secretary Ernest Bevin had the busmen's committee's powers revoked. The committee's defeat set back the chances of major reductions in the working week throughout British industry, but a fresh agreement later in 1937 brought an eight-hour maximum duty period. The strike cost the Board £0.7 million in lost revenue and 86 million passenger journeys, despite 60 per cent more business going to trams and trolleybuses and 100 per cent more by Underground. It dented a rising curve of traffic which had been built up from 1933/34, when 5,976 buses and coaches carried 1.9 billion passengers. In 1935/36, 6,298 buses and coaches carried 2.1 billion passengers, but figures dipped in the strike year to 2 billion passengers in 6,454 buses. In 1938/39, when the fleet had dropped to 6,389, 2.2 billion passengers were carried.

In addition to its motorbuses, the Board also inherited 2,630 trams from London County Council, Croydon, East Ham, and West Ham County Boroughs, Barking, Bexley, Erith, Ilford, and Walthamstow Urban District Councils, and from the Underground-associated London United, Metropolitan Electric, and South Metropolitan Electric Tramways. Trams carried 1 billion passengers in 1933/34 over 327 route miles, but the last LCC car had been built in 1932, and the combine's 100 advanced Feltham cars had been built a year earlier. The tram's day had passed. However, instead of replacing them with motorbuses, the Board safeguarded its investment in electric generating equipment and overhead lines by switching to trolleybuses. This also reduced the Board's total dependence upon imported fuel for its services.

London United had 61 trolleybuses running over 18 route miles in South-West London when the Board took over. A Twickenham—Teddington service, which started in May 1931, proved 15 per cent cheaper to operate than the obsolete trams, and paved the way for the planned conversion of the entire tram system to trolleybuses. The original 61 trolleys all were six-wheeler AECs, with 56 or 74 seats and, following trials with a 73-seat six-wheel and a 60-seat four-wheel AEC, the Board settled on the larger vehicle to meet its needs for high-capacity buses.

Another 95 route miles were added following the granting of Parliamentary powers in 1934, and the 1935-40 New Works Programme, which was taken up mainly with Underground and suburban railway extensions, included another 148 miles of trolleybus routes in its £40 million budget.

By 1939, trolleybus route mileage had risen to 236, and 1,411 vehicles were carrying 571 million passengers. Tram route mileage had fallen to 135, and 1,316 cars were carrying 516 million passengers. Had it not been for the outbreak of war, which stopped the trolley in its tracks in 1940, all of London's trams would have gone by 1942. London trolleybuses owed little to the design of their motorbus fleetmates, but the fleet, which was built in almost equal numbers by AEC and Leyland, did reflect the Board's advanced thinking. In 1937, the first of 179 chassisless trolleys, with the chassis and body integrated into one much stronger structure, was built. Although popular in the United States, integral construction had to wait another 35 years before gaining widespread acceptance in Britain.

The Board also bought 26 AECs with unit construction bodies. This simpler solution to the rigidity problem, which also was tried on the underfloor-engined Green Line coaches described in Chapter Seven, involved the body being built directly on to a lightweight chassis.

In its last year of peacetime, the Board became increasingly pre-occupied with war, and in spring 1939 an air raid precautions exercise was mounted at Cricklewood Garage. Personnel were trained to combat gas, incendiary and high explosive bombs, and to render first aid. A Green Line coach had already been converted into a ten-stretcher ambulance, and nearly 400 were similarly adapted within hours of the coach services' withdrawal on August 31 that year. September 1 1939 found 4,170 buses and 900 trams and trolleybuses at work on the start of a four day evacuation of half a million Londoners, mostly children, to 'safe' areas. That exercise, which was completed without incident, marked the start of a period when the Board's reputation for organisation and planning would be put to the test.

Right *Towards new horizons. A General AEC Renown 664, one of 199 single-deckers nicknamed Scooters, climbs London's Muswell Hill, passing would-be home buyers in April 1931* (London Transport).

SYDNEY BOWYER & Co
FIRE LOSS ASSESSORS
AUCTIONEERS SURVEYORS VALUERS
TUDOR 5368
SYDNEY BOWYER & Co
VALUATIONS FOR PROBATE.
HOUSE & ESTATE AGENTS.
ENTRANCE NEXT DOOR.
SYDNEY BOWYER & Co
ESTATE A
HOUSE, LAND AND ESTATE
SYDNEY BOWYER & C
111
MUSWELL HILL BDY
GENERAL
LT1017
GO 617
ESTATE OFFICES
OPPOSITE
HOUSES!!!
SYDNEY BOWYER & Co.
THE PERTH DYE WORKS
MADELINE CARROLL
FRENCH LEAVE
CULLEN LAND
THE CONVIC
CODE

Proud employees of East London-based Gordon Omnibus Company pose with the company's Dodson-bodied Maudslay Mentor ML7C2 double-decker. Additional summer ventilation was provided through a sliding roof. The Gordon business was taken over by the LPTB in December 1933, and the bus was sold early in 1936 (D.W.K. Jones).

The sole vehicle in E.G. Hope's Pembroke fleet, a Birch-bodied Regent, survived the decade, and was lost with other stored buses when Peckham premises were bombed in 1940 (D.W.K. Jones).

The Westminster Omnibus Company insisted on having the driver of this 1933 Sunbeam Sikh exposed to the elements. A windscreen, it was believed, would cause draughts and harm his health, so a metal cowl and storm apron were specified instead. LPTB sold the bus soon after the company was taken over in July 1934 (J.F. Higham).

This AEC Renown began life as a 50-seat Green Line coach, when coach traffic was booming, but it was soon relegated to country bus work, to join forward-entrance STL-type Regents (D.W.K. Jones).

Right *Jubilee year in Park Lane. A former Tilling Regent, new in 1933, leads a mid-1920s NS-type against a backdrop of a patriotically decorated Cumberland Hotel* (London Transport).

Inset *One of the smallest buses to find its way into LPTB hands was this 14-seat Birch-bodied Bean taken over in July 1932 by General along with eight other small buses in Mrs N.F.A. Sayers' Harrow-based Royal Highlander fleet. It was sold in 1936, when it was five years old* (D.W.K. Jones).

Mirror
JOHN BUCHAN WRITES
36
MARBLE ARCH
VICTORIA STN
CAMBERWELL GRN
NEW +
LEWISHAM HIGH RD
Mirror
LIFE OF THE KING
CRUISES
AGF 827

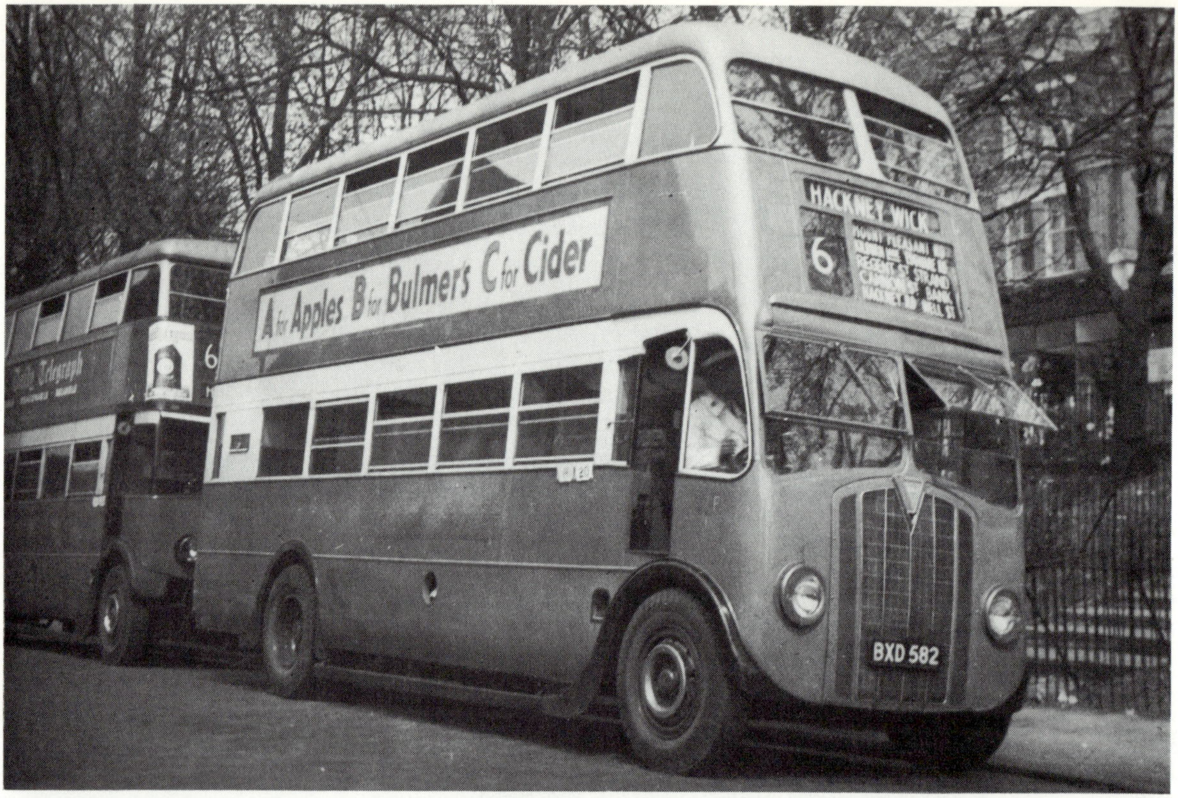
A for Apples B for Bulmers C for Cider
HACKNEY WICK
6
BXD 582

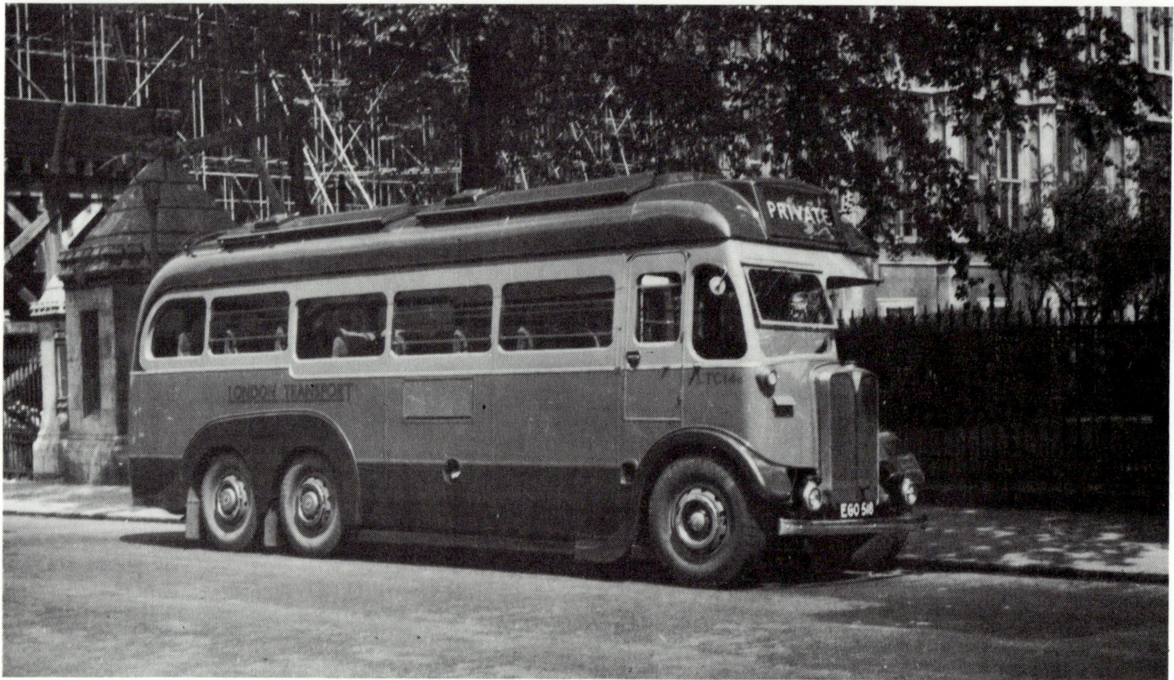

PRIVATE
LONDON TRANSPORT

Above left *An early attempt at streamlining the standard LPTB bus was the STF, a fully-fronted 1935 AEC Regent. It soon lost many of its distinguishing features, but it showed the way the style-conscious organisation wanted to go* (J.F. Higham).

Left *Ottaway par excellence. The Chiswick design team's skill for producing practical, but advanced, styles is evident in one of 24 Renown coaches built in 1937* (D.W.K. Jones).

Above *Typical of over 200 Leylands which LPTB acquired with independent businesses was this 1932 Titan TD2 with Dodson 53-seat bodywork owned by East London-based Pro Bono Publico Ltd* (J.F. Higham).

Right *A sizeable fleet of Leyland Cubs was bought for the less busy routes. The chassis were built at Leyland's Kingston-upon-Thames factory* (D.W.K. Jones).

13
DEL MONTE
GOOD BYE ISOLATION!
LONDON BDG STN
STRAND
CANNON STREET
DLU 348

IMPERIAL
RAINHAM
Imperial
11
VX 9932

Above left *One hundred Leyland Titan TD4s were supplied in coronation year, and had chassis and body features borrowed from the more numerous AECs in the fleet* (J.F. Higham).

Left *Among 11 single-deckers taken over in November 1934 with the Imperial Bus Services fleet of A.E. Blane, of Romford, was this Morris Commercial Dictator with 26-seat Metcalfe body. The company ran two services in the Romford area* (D.W.K. Jones).

Above *The RT, unveiled in 1939, stood head and shoulders above anything built for service elsewhere. Its glory was to come a decade later, when a family of nearly 7,000 was being built up* (London Transport).

WHITBREAD'S ALE & STOUT
FREE TRAVEL
NASH ESTATE
NASH ESTATE TRANSPORT.
VICTORIA
GHOSTS
OLIVER LODGE
BANK
HAMMERSMITH

Left *Eight 20-seat Cub observation coaches were bought for an inter-station service which started in October 1936. It connected Kings Cross, St Pancras, Euston, Marylebone and Paddington main-line express trains to Scotland, Wales, the Midlands, North and West of England with Continental boat trains and southbound expresses from Victoria and Waterloo. The fare was 1/- (5p)* (London Transport).

Inset left *In some cases, estate developers provided free feeder bus services until LPTB stepped in. This 1939 Bedford WTB was run by T.F. Nash construction at developments in Hayes (Middlesex) and Romford (Essex)* (D.W.K. Jones).

Below left *The combine on show. Trams, LT-type Renown and underground station at Hammersmith in August 1936* (London Transport).

Above *Two trolleybuses, a Brush-bodied Leyland on the left and a Metro-Cammell-bodied AEC 664T on the right, at Bexleyheath in May 1936. Both are on the Woolwich—Dartford section of the system which opened in November the previous year* (London Transport).

Above right *Independents loved their Gilfords, which were cheap, but powerful machines available at an attractive price. This 168OT with 30-seat body by the Gilford-owned Wycombe company, was new in 1932, and was photographed in Romford two years later, soon after the Edward Hillman fleet passed into Green Line hands* (D.W.K. Jones).

Right *Four standard STL-type Regents and two LT-type Renowns help make up the busy 1930s atmosphere in this view of the Strand at the Aldwych* (London Transport).

DEATH TO THE SICK ELEPHANTS

Business on Britain's municipal buses boomed in the 1930s, thanks largely to mammoth tramway replacement schemes and the beginning of urban renewal in many towns and cities. They carried about 100 million passengers extra each year, and the number of municipally-owned buses doubled from around 5,500 in 1930 to 11,000 in 1939. Given that most municipal undertakings were in the traditional industrial areas of Northern England, the Midlands, and South Wales, that growth was all the more impressive, as it occurred against a background of the trade depression and heavy unemployment. But, while operators did feel the pinch—Birmingham lost 4 million passengers between 1929 and 1930 owing to factory closures and short-time working in industry, and another industrial municipality reported that the means test, begun in November 1931, reduced its weekly takings by £2 per bus—the effect was barely noticeable generally.

It was the electric tram, rendered obsolete by great advances in bus design, which fell by the wayside. The Royal Commission on Transport, which reported in 1931, reflected the views of many when it said trams caused unnecessary congestion and were a considerable danger to the public. It proposed that no more tramways be constructed and said that, while it was impossible to set a date for their complete disappearance, they should nonetheless vanish from Britain's streets. Progressive opinion was stacked heavily against the tram, accusing it of being slow and noisy, and too inflexible to share urban roads with increasing numbers of motor vehicles. In an age when a brave new world held more attraction than nostalgia, J.B. Priestley commented on a Birmingham tram ride, saying: 'There is something depressing about the way in which a tram lumbers and groans and grinds along, like a sick elephant'.

The sick elephants went to their graveyard. Over 70 tram systems, more than half of them municipally-owned, closed between 1930 and 1939, and many others were well on the way to their end. Such systems as those at Stockton-on-Tees, Rochdale, Derby, Nottingham and Halifax closed, and scrapping programmes were well in hand in Huddersfield, Newcastle, Birmingham and Coventry. The results achieved reinforced the anti-tram case. Chester reported a 73 per cent increase in revenue when it bought 16 AEC buses to replace its trams in 1930, and Wigan claimed that when it replaced trams with buses on the 4½-mile Ashton-in-Makerfield route the same year, that the journey time had been reduced from 40 to only 10 minutes. Burnley, Colne and Nelson reported in 1934 that it increased business on its Barrowford routes by 30 per cent when 52-seat Leyland Titans replaced single-deck trams, extra passengers being former pedestrians and cyclists. The working man had still to become a motorist.

However, all these results pale into insignificance against the performance of Manchester Corporation, whose general manager, Stuart Pilcher, became almost a god to the tram-to-bus movement. Despite 23 years' experience in charge of the heavily tram-biased Aberdeen and Edinburgh transport systems, 47-year-old Pilcher was still young and imaginative enough to appreciate the potential of the bus, and his influence upon others was dramatic. He gave the tram its last chance, commissioning a modern vehicle for Manchester which bore his name, but even that failed to meet bus competition, and Pilcher reported that, on the Altrincham route, passengers preferred buses, even though their fares were 50 per cent higher than those on trams. When 60 50-seat lowbridge Crossley Condor and Leyland Titan TD1 double-deckers replaced 66 single-deck trams on the city's partially single-track route 53 in April 1930, the results vindicated Pilcher's faith in the future of the bus. Seating capacity on the route went up by 13.6 per cent, average speed rose from 9 mph to 11 mph and the service generated £17,891 extra revenue.

By 1932, a continuing programme of tram replacement, as track fell due to renewal, had turned a £13,000 loss into a £36,000 profit, and the city accelerated the programme as it set its sights on the withdrawal of its last tram in 1942. The war only delayed that by seven years.

If the bus was making a clean sweep in Manchester, it had a fight on its hands in Edinburgh, Glasgow and Liverpool. The Scottish capital confined most of its buses to tram-feeder routes and, although it increased its fleet from 129 in 1930 to 210 in 1939, it slipped from sixth to eleventh place among municipal fleets. Glasgow, which continued to modernise its tram fleet into the early 1950s, remained convinced that trams were better equipped to deal with large crowds, and fought off pre-war moves to introduce trolleybuses. On the other hand, it did develop new bus routes to serve the expanding city and, although Manchester overtook it as second largest municipal operator, it more than doubled its fleet from 245 in 1930 to 595 in 1939.

Liverpool was another story. It clung resolutely to the tram throughout the 1930s, building over 400 new vehicles and extending the system, mainly on reserved sleeper track. In 1931, it considered its 200 buses to be 'a drain on the finances of the undertaking', and two years later, when tramway extension was swinging into top notch and bus losses of £84,000 compared with tram profits of £35,000, buses were withdrawn from areas where they competed with trams—notably in the city centre—and the fleet dropped to only 120 vehicles. New services began to be developed on the outskirts from 1935, but buses continued to carry only about an eighth of the traffic handled by the ever-expanding tram system and the 160-strong fleet—fourth largest municipal bus operator in 1930—had fallen to eighteenth place by 1939, overtaken even by Portsmouth, Plymouth, Nottingham and Hull.

For others, a compromise lay between the radical policies of Manchester and the conservatism of Liverpool. That was the trolleybus, which as well as being quieter and simpler for redundant tram drivers to control, was cheaper and more flexible to operate than the tram. And although the tram track often was worn out, trolleybuses could use electric generating equipment and overhead wire installations which still had years of life ahead of them. As the international situation deteriorated and supplies of foreign fuel oil looked uncertain, the political case for the trolleybus gained strength. The Coal Utilisation Council lobbied operators who were planning to replace trams and, in 1938, Transport Minister Leslie Burgin underlined Government concern when he told a London audience: 'Just as I am desirous that the tram should be removed and its place taken by a bus, so I think that the bus should be a trolleybus, using an equivalent output of electricity generated by an equivalent expenditure on coal.'

While the older trolleybus systems at York, Keighley, Ramsbottom, Wigan and Chesterfield were abandoned during the 1930s and replaced by motorbuses, 15 new systems began in the same period and, by 1939, 29 municipalities were running over 1,600 vehicles. Huddersfield led with a fleet of 140 and was followed by Bradford, Nottingham, Wolverhampton, Bournemouth, Newcastle and Porstmouth, all with 100 or more. Birmingham ran a small fleet and even Manchester, against Pilcher's professional judgement, started trolleybus services in 1938. Belfast, the only municipal operator on either side of the Irish border, began an experimental service in the same year with 14 buses and ordered 114 more in 1939.

The upsurge in demand for new trolleybuses was satisfied mainly by motorbus manufacturers who co-operated with electrical contractors experienced in supplying equipment for trams. Such low volume trolleybus builders as Guy, Karrier and Ransomes were joined in 1930 by AEC, who built English Electric-powered models based on Regent, Renown and Regal bus chassis, and in 1931 by Leyland, who used GEC equipment in Titan and, later, Titanic and Tiger-based chassis, and by Sunbeam, who had purpose-built chassis with Metropolitan Vickers equipment. Crossley and Daimler also used Metro-Vick equipment when they entered the market in 1935 and 1936 respectively.

Buses, both motor and trolley, were also needed to meet the need for transport as inner cities were redeveloped and new housing was created on the outskirts. Manchester's Wythenshawe estate, nine miles from the city centre, had over 6,000 houses by 1935 and sparked off many new services. And in Leeds, where a five-year plan to demolish 30,000 slums and rehouse 110,000 inhabitants began in 1934, housing planners called in municipal busmen at an early stage.

Coventry's constant growth, especially after the Government established 'shadow' aircraft component factories in the area, forced housing to spread out to accommodate the influx of new families. From running 62 buses and carrying 26 million passengers in 1933, Coventry had 125 buses in 1939 and carried 57 million passengers. Even its tram system, cut down to only ten route miles by March 1938, was running a greater mileage to handle extra traffic and, in 1939, the city broke new ground by operating four-wheel 60-seat Daimler

COG5/60 double-deckers in place of 56-seaters found elsewhere.

However, the busmen did not get it all without some penalties. Birmingham transport manager Alfred Baker complained throughout the 1930s that, although buses handled extra business, there was little money in it. Comparatively few residents of the new estates used buses for journeys other than to and from work (the suburbs had their own pubs and cinemas), and journeys to work were often at a discount fare. Buses frequently ran empty in one direction and 75 per cent of the fleet was out of action outside peak periods. In 1938, Mr Baker pointed out that 112 buses were needed for the Outer Circle service between 7 am and 9 am, and only 26 an hour later, and housing estate services which needed 73 buses before 9 am, needed only 13 after that. The seeds of a post-war problem were beginning to be sown.

There were other ways that municipalities, unlike companies, could protect their investments, an extreme solution being the Glasgow Corporation Act of 1930, which gave the city's buses and trams a monopoly of all local traffic. Companies, including SMT group members which had been running into the city from the mid-1920s, put up a struggle, but lost thousands of passengers as a result of the Act, and some had to dismiss employees. Nottingham, which was in the throes of its tram-to-trolleybus conversion scheme, secured similar protection against outside operators; but when Colchester Corporation tried to get a 25 per cent share of operators' takings within its boundaries in 1931, the Eastern Traffic Commissioners told it to go away and think again.

Rather than keep companies out of their territories, other municipalities were encouraged by Traffic Commissioners to reach civilised agreements with them, along the lines of the Plymouth agreement in Chapter One. Newcastle was running jointly with United Auto and Tynemouth by 1932 and, from January 1933, Southend introduced a new pattern of services, taking over five routes run by Westcliff-on-Sea Motor Services, Edwards Hall Motors and Borough Services, but agreeing not to make full use of its trolleybus powers in other parts of the town.

In Hull, the Corporation reached a deal with East Yorkshire Motor Services from 1934, whereby mileage and receipts were shared within defined areas and, a year later, the two operators jointly purchased the Sharpe's Motors business running in the town. Other authorities preferred to sell or lease their small undertakings to area companies and, under such deals, the Kilmarnock fleet passed to SMT in 1932, Perth's went to Alexander in 1934 and Gloucester's to Bristol Tramways in 1936. West Yorkshire reached special deals with Keighley and York Corporations to take over their bus undertakings in 1932 and 1934. A joint management company, with three corporation and four company representatives, took over at Keighley with successful enough results to move the council to say in 1935: 'When we compare the dismal financial returns of the old corporation trams and trolleybuses with the figures before us now, we see an absolute vindication of the value of private enterprise in the management of business and industry'. In York, the company managed services on the corporation's behalf.

Under comparable arrangements, municipal trams were replaced by company buses where local authorities either were unwilling to invest in buses or trolleybuses, or failed to gain bus operating powers. Alexander buses replaced Kirkcaldy's trams in 1931, SMT buses replaced Ayr trams in 1932 and Dover's trams were replaced by East Kent buses in January 1937, following ratepayers' rejection of a trolleybus proposal for the town. Bristol's trams, bought from the Tilling group in 1937 for £1.125 million, were replaced from May 1938 by a fleet of 356 Bristol double-deckers owned by Bristol Joint Services, a corporation/Bristol Tramways joint company.

Carlisle City Council plans to take over company trams and buses in 1931 were thwarted by the Northern Traffic Commissioners, who refused the council a licence and forced it to cancel an order for 59 buses which would have replaced the trams. Instead, Ribble took over and scrapped the trams.

It took Brighton until April 1 1939 to become a bus operator, by which time it was the only municipal transport operator running only trams. It spent the entire decade trying to reach an accommodation with Tilling, who operated bus services in the town (from 1935 as Brighton, Hove and District) and was tripped up by various obstacles on the way. A Bill to establish a Brighton District Transport Board was withdrawn in 1931 after Brighton ratepayers rejected the proposal in a 23 per cent poll. Plans for a joint Brighton/Tilling company, and later for a York-style takeover, came to naught.

Matters started to move in 1936 when the Wolverhampton and Sheffield transport managers, Owen Silvers and Arthur Fearnley—the latter something of a tram replacement consultant in the 1930s—recommended a joint agreement. The result was a 21-year revenue pooling deal, in which the company got 72.5 per cent and the corporation 27.5 per cent. A fleet of 65 corporation-owned AEC motorbuses and trolleybuses replaced the trams

Plymouth Corporation bought 14 of these Leyland Titan TD3s with lowbridge Weymann bodies in 1934 as part of a tramway replacement programme begun in October 1930. Trials conducted with this vehicle, No 21, convinced the city of the merits of diesel engines and torque converter transmission (Leyland Vehicles).

between April and September 1939. Eight trolleybuses also went to the company, but were stored until after the war.

While several municipal undertakings also considered mergers and joint working agreements, relatively few put their plans into practice. The Burnley, Colne and Nelson undertakings were merged in 1933 and replaced their trams within two years. A similar amalgamation of the Blackburn, Darwen and Accrington undertakings in East Lancashire was proposed in August 1939, but got lost in the aftermath of the outbreak of war.

In South Wales, Merthyr Tydfil, Aberdare, Caerphilly, Pontypridd, Rhondda and Gellygaer councils considered setting up a joint transport undertaking in 1930 to safeguard their interests before the traffic courts. They proposed that Bedwas and Machen and the West Monmouthshire Joint Omnibus Board (Bedwellty and Mynyddislwyn Urban District Councils) would join them and that an agreement be reached with Cardiff. Nothing further came of the plan, but several joint service agreements were reached between the municipalities, including Cardiff, and with companies.

More serious efforts were made to establish a joint board in South East Lancashire and East Cheshire—foreshadowing the events of the late-1960s—after Oldham Corporation proposed a merger of the municipal bus and tram systems around Manchester in 1931. The idea, which was influenced by the progress of the London Passenger Transport Bill, was for a more efficient system to be run, with fewer vehicles, cheaper fares and more through services. There also was the suggestion that the savings could be used to finance tube railways in Greater Manchester.

Initial talks resulted in a £10 million scheme, announced in 1934, for the Manchester, Ashton-under-Lyne, Bolton, Bury, Oldham, Rochdale, Salford, Stockport, and Stalybridge, Hyde, Mossley, and Duckinfield Joint Board undertakings to be merged, bringing 13,600 employees and 2,400 buses and trams into uniform control. Wigan and Leigh were omitted from the scheme because their services did not run into Manchester. By mid-1936, only Manchester, Salford and Oldham were still interested in the plan and a conference early in 1937 involving all 11 municipalities and company operators Ribble, North Western, the independent Lancashire United Transport and Power Company and the railways, proved to be the scheme's swansong. By then, the railways had said no more electrification could be contemplated in Manchester until a London-style board was established.

Around the time the SELEC scheme died, Stoke-on-Trent City Council, supported by Newcastle-under-Lyme, sponsored a private Bill to establish a

North Staffordshire Passenger Transport Board to take over the 250 buses operated by Potteries Motor Traction and a similar number run by independent concerns. The Board, modelled on the London and Northern Ireland Boards, was to have been given a monopoly and supported by ratepayers. Independents, feeling no doubt that they may as well be hung for a municipal sheep as a Potteries lamb, made tentative agreements to sell out on the basis of £4,400 per bus, but the combine company joined Stafford and Crewe Corporations in opposing the Bill. Midland Red traffic manager Cecil Power, speaking as chairman of the Birmingham Horse and Motor Vehicle Owners' Association, described the Bill's sponsors as 'a group of autocratic municipal administrators suffering from an acute attack of megalomania', and there were other criticisms of it being a short cut to nationalisation. The Bill was thrown out of the House of Commons by 163 votes to 108 in March 1937.

Calls for a transport board on Merseyside began to be heard in 1936. Tram-style protectionism, this time aimed at the Mersey railway and ferries, was keeping buses out of the two-year-old Mersey Tunnel, and the Wirral municipalities of Birkenhead and Wallasey were particularly keen that something be done. A study was commissioned by the Merseyside Co-ordination Committee, but its authors, municipal finance expert Arthur Collins, the LPTB's Frank Pick and the ubiquitous Mr Fearnley, stopped short of recommending a board. They proposed an experimental tunnel bus, maximum co-operation (especially on fares) and a possible merger of the Wirral undertakings.

In March 1937, the Royal Commission on Local Government proposed that the Ministry of Transport conduct an inquiry into a Tyneside Passenger Transport Board as part of the unification of local government in the region, and Transport Minister Burgin started to consult local authorities later in the year. Northern General considered the Board unnecessary, but Newcastle's transport committee chairman had told the Royal Commission: 'I think a transport board is bound to come'. It was—30 years later.

In the meantime, municipal busmen had to bear the burdens of the inevitable slide into war and many vehicles and their premises were adapted to cope with the expected onslaught. Buses were converted into ambulances and—from 1938 onwards—staff in many parts were trained in gas decontamination. Leeds central bus station, opened in August 1938, incorporated an underground air raid shelter for 150, and Coventry, appreciating its vulnerability as a 'shadow' factory city, had special 25,000-gallon fuel tanks built in sand-filled concrete chambers away from its garage. Suddenly, mergers, expansion and the finer points of co-ordination became an irrelevance.

The final traces of Preston's tramlines were being covered in January 1936, when this photograph was taken. The replacement buses were built locally, Titan TD3c chassis by Leyland and lowbridge bodies by English Electric (Leyland Vehicles).

Above *Wigan's last trams ran in 1931. Of these two Leyland Titans, the leading example is a TD5 with a style of bodywork introduced in 1938* (J.F. Higham).

Below *Manchester's route 53 conversion in April 1930 convinced the city of the merits of the bus against the tram. The Leyland Titan TD1s which replaced the single-deck trams had 48-seat lowbridge bodies with sunken gangways on both sides of the top deck, and examples in this view were bodied by Strachan and by Short* (Leyland Vehicles).

Above *Birkenhead was a much more enthusiastic bus operator than Liverpool, across the Mersey. Here, Leyland-bodied Titan TD1s and relaxing crews await ferry passengers at Woodside terminal in September 1931* (Leyland Vehicles).

Left *Edinburgh's reluctance to make large scale use of buses resulted in it buying more single-deckers than many municipal undertakings. This Weymann-bodied rear-entrance Daimler COG5 was typical of the buses bought by the Scottish capital* (Robert Grieves collection).

Above *The Northern Traffic Commissioners agreed to protect the Teesside Railless Traction Board's trolleybus services in 1931, provided it was modernised within a year. The result was that eight 32-seater Ransomes vehicles (right) were bought in 1932 to replace the ten Cleveland Car Company 28-seaters with English Electric bodies which had maintained services from 1919* (Cleveland Transit, Middlesbrough).

Right *A fleet of Thornycrofts, like this Martin-bodied BC, helped Bournemouth Corporation boost its revenue in 1930. They provided limited stop services along all of the tram routes, leaving the trams to carry local traffic, and saving time for passengers boarding the trams* (D.W.K. Jones).

Top *Wallasey bought this Burlingham-bodied Leyland Cub KPZ4 in 1939* (Roy Marshall).

Above *Douglas Corporation managed to squeeze 28 years' service from this 1939 AEC Regent with Northern Counties bodywork* (A. Moyes).

Right *The only Leyland-GEC FA3B trolleybuses built were used on Birmingham's small system. They were based on Titan TD1 chassis, complete with dummy radiators, and had 48-seat Short Brothers bodies* (Leyland Vehicles).

NECHELLS
DV 4010
LEWISS

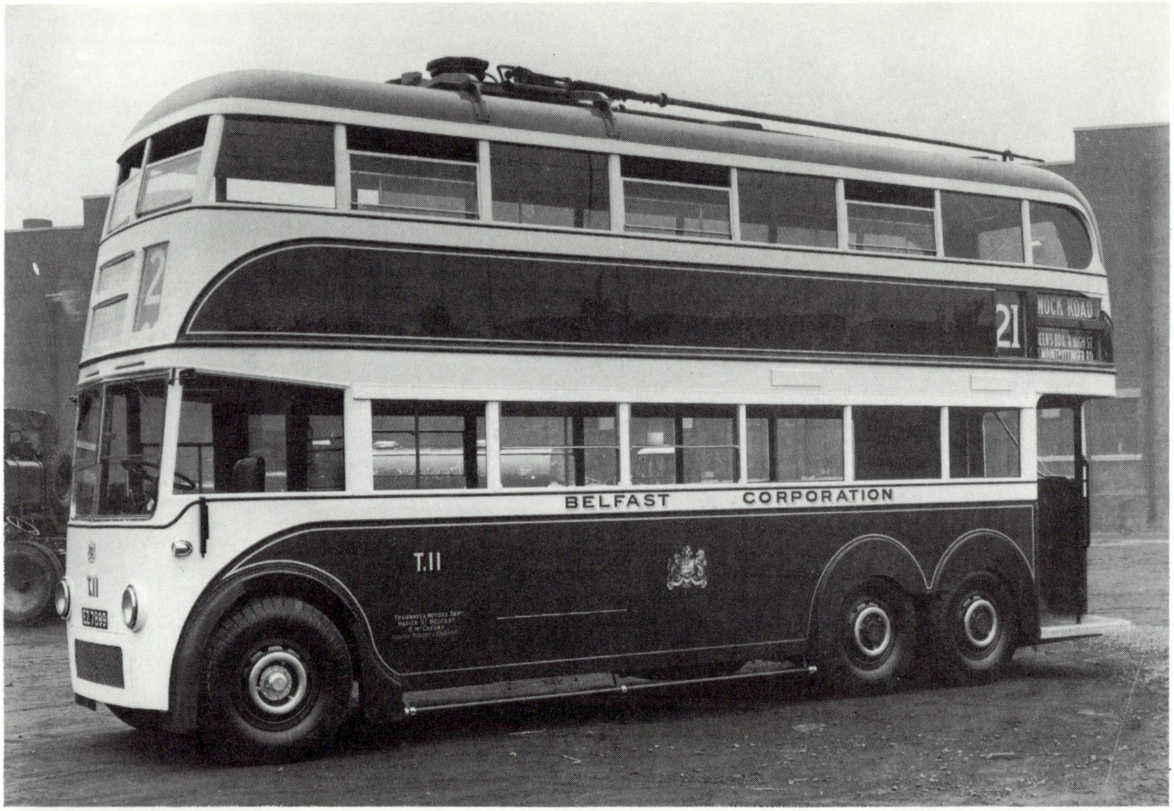
21
BELFAST CORPORATION
T.11

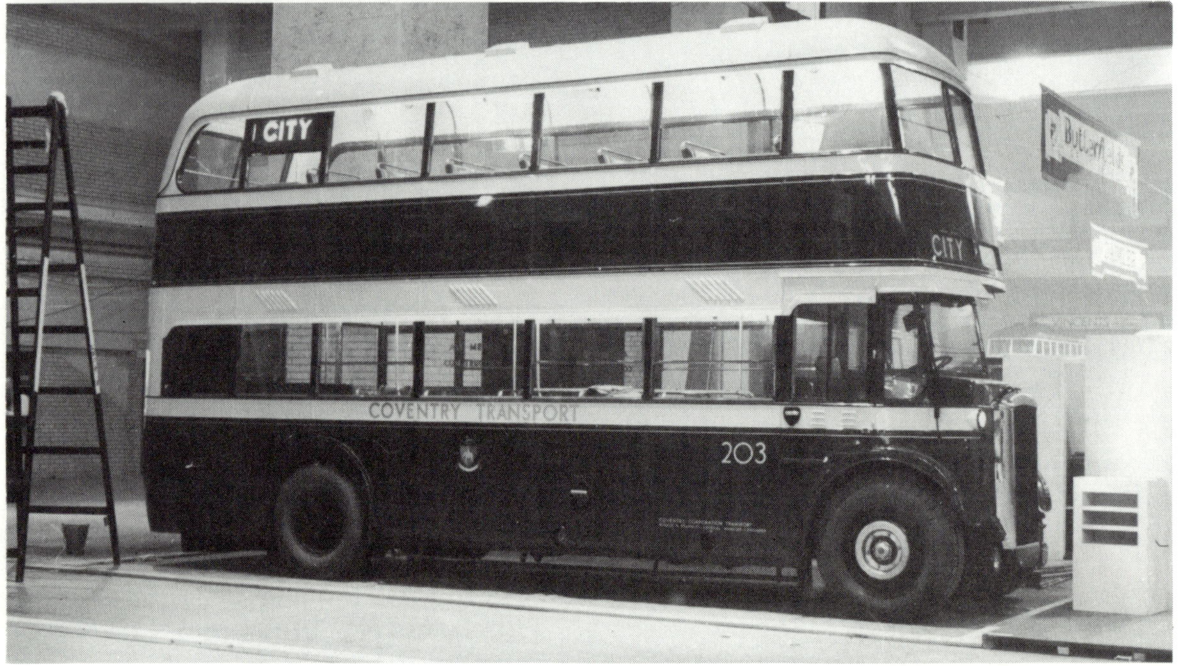

CITY
CITY
COVENTRY TRANSPORT
203

Above left *Belfast began an experimental trolleybus service in 1938, using 14 assorted AEC, Leyland, Crossley, Karrier, Guy, Daimler, and Sunbeam double-deckers. The Leylands were bodied by the chassis builder, and resembled contemporary London trolleys* (Leyland Vehicles).

Left *A Brush-bodied Daimler COA6, new in 1937, of the type with which Coventry Corporation met the transport needs of the growing West Midlands city* (Alan Millar collection).

Above *The Stockton-on-Tees fleet included this Daimler COG5 with Craven bodywork* (Robert C. Davis collection).

Right *An English Electric-bodied 48-seater Leyland Titan TD3 operated by Barrow-in-Furness Corporation* (Robert C. Davis).

RESERVED
JA 7589
JA 7600
188
2

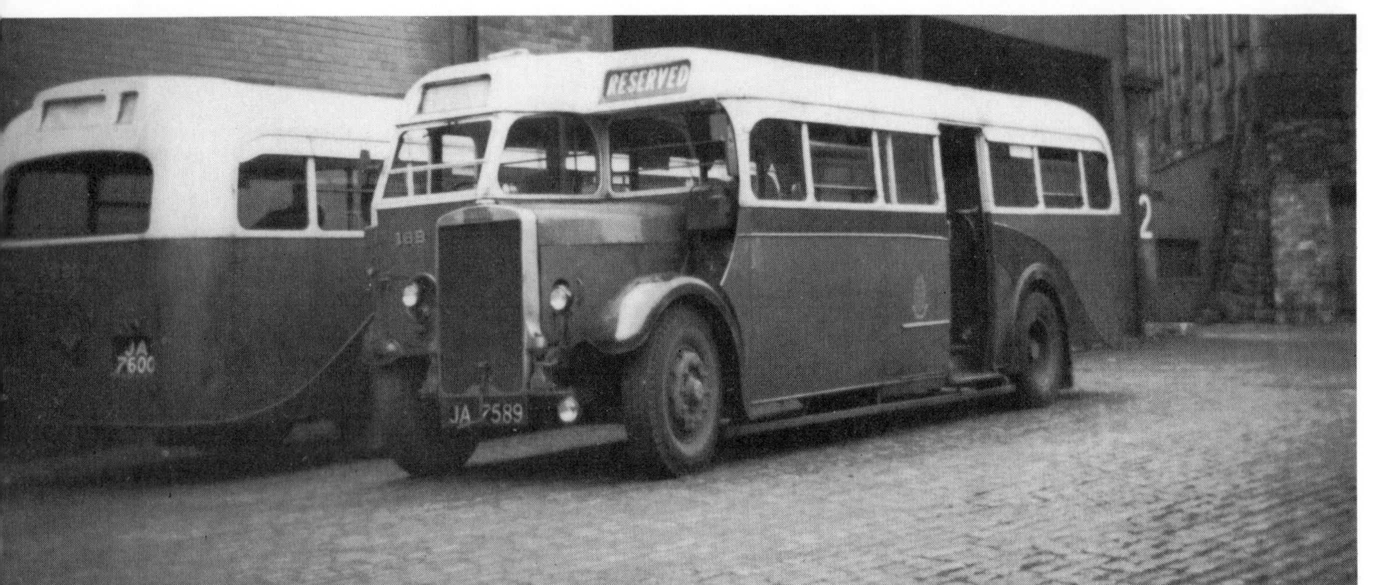

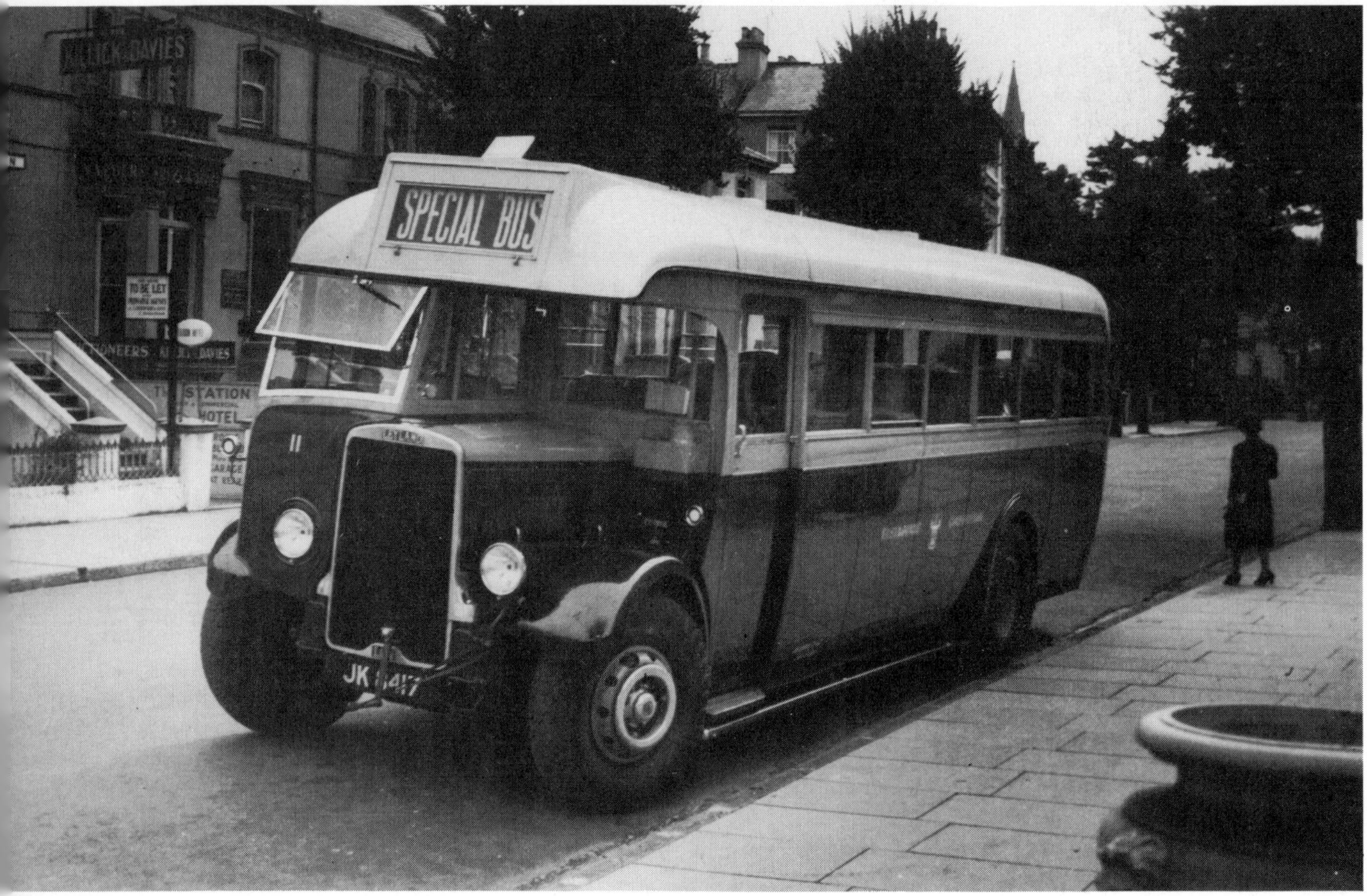
SPECIAL BUS
KILLICK & DAVIES
TO BE LET
STATION
HOTEL

Above left *The SELEC undertaking would have included Stockport's bus fleet. Nearest the camera is an English Electric-bodied Leyland Tiger TS7, new in 1936, while the vehicle behind is a similar 1937 Tiger TS8* (A. Moyes).

Left *Eastbourne remained faithful to petrol-engined buses throughout the 1930s, believing that they created a better environment than noisier diesels would. This 1939 Leyland Lion LT8 32-seater was requisitioned for war service and did not return to the Sussex resort* (D.W.K. Jones).

Above *A Bristol single-decker operated by Lowestoft Corporation, one of the smallest undertakings in the hands of a local council* (J.F. Higham).

Right *Newcastle's first trolleybus route, along West Road, began in 1935. A Metro Cammell-bodied Karrier E6A (left) passes a Brush-bodied AEC 664T* (Robert C. Davis collection).

Background photograph *A Manchester Corporation Bristol B Superbus, new in 1928, at London Road Station on a route from there to Victoria Station. The bus lasted until 1937* (Greater Manchester Transport Museum Society).

Inset *Sheer 1930s indulgence. A star of the 1935 Commercial Motor Show was this Leeds Corporation AEC Regent with highly streamlined and fully-fronted Roe bodywork. No more were built* (Charles H. Roe Ltd).

You'll feel you've had
something worth drinking
when you've had a
GUINNESS

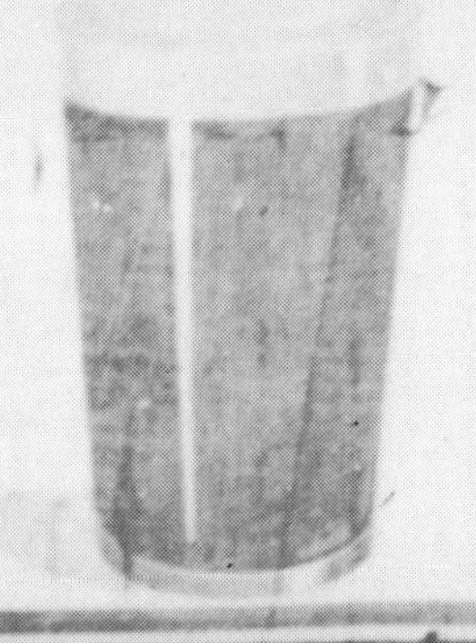

VICTORIA STATION
LONDON ROAD STATION

A
GUINNESS
A DAY

123

JOHN GREENHALGH
STOCKPORT
ACE
OF
PRESERVES

REVOLUTION BENEATH THE BONNET

There are days which punctuate history and mark the start of a whole course of new development. For the British bus industry Sunday March 9 1930 was one of those days, as it was then that Sheffield Corporation became the first operator to place a diesel-engined bus in service. The spark-ignition petrol engine, by then engineered to a fine degree of efficiency, but prone to high fuel consumption, soon lost its predominance and the economics of bus operation were changed.

That Sheffield's pioneering bus, a 35-seat Karrier WL6 six-wheeler, had a German Mercedes-Benz 77 bhp engine fitted in place of its Dorman petrol engine was hardly surprising. A German, Dr Rudolph Diesel, had developed his first compression ignition engine, to run on coal dust, some 40 years earlier. German manufacturer MAN had built the first diesel engine in 1897; and Mercedes had imported two diesel-engined lorries to Britain in 1928, giving the country's commercial vehicle operators their first chance of using the more economical power unit. The diesel, or 'oil engine' as purists termed it at the time in deference to the actual nature of Diesel's invention, had an enthusiastic British promoter in one Major W.H. Goddard. He acted as a consultant on the Sheffield project and later established Pelican Engineering, a Leeds-based company which re-equipped buses and lorries with Gardner diesels.

Goddard waxed eloquently about the performance of the Karrier, which clocked up 1,000 miles a week on the Sheffield—Doncaster route, and returned an average of 11 mpg at 4¼d (2p) per gallon. Within days of its entry into service, he said: 'No one has complained, no one's clothes have been soiled, the bus is a very great success . . . there is no smoke or fumes, and no sign of creeping of the oil anywhere'. And commenting on the reduced need for gear-changing, and the health-giving absence of petrol fumes, he claimed that 'driver Godbere says the engine will give him an extra ten years of life'.

As happens so often with pioneers, the Sheffield bus remained unique. Mercedes did offer its N2 bonneted single-decker on the British market, complete with its 85 bhp OM58 diesel and Request Services of Preston bought two with 26-seat Burlingham bus bodies in 1931; but British diesel developments, import controls and the swing away from small buses prevented the German company from making any headway. It was left to the Nottinghamshire independent, Barton Transport, to set the trend when, a few days after the Sheffield bus took to the road, it placed its own diesel-engined single-decker on the Nottingham—Coalville route. Thomas Henry Barton had long been interested in the diesel principle and, when Manchester's L. Gardner and Sons launched their 65 bhp 4L2 four-cylinder marine diesel in 1929, he was quick to identify its possibilities as a bus engine.

Within a year, Barton was running four diesel buses. Two had 4L2 engines and were returning 20 mpg with negligible engine wear. Another had a five-cylinder Gardner 5L2, which returned 18 mpg, and the fourth had a Stamford-built Blackstone engine. All carried the legend 'British Fuel Oil Bus. No petrol, no danger.' on their sides and the company claimed as a useful side benefit their ability to negotiate flooded roads. But it was their favourable running costs which impressed the most; not only was fuel consumption about half that of petrol buses but, unlike petrol, diesel fuel was untaxed and cost about 5d less per gallon. Walsall Corporation fitted a 4L2 into a four-year old Dennis E single-decker in 1930, but it was another Goddard project which next hit the headlines. He was involved closely in the installation of a six-cylinder 75 bhp Gardner 6L2 in a 48-seat Crossley Condor double-decker for the Leeds undertaking. It entered service in September 1930 and had been followed by similar vehicles with Sheffield and Manchester before the year ended. Events were moving very quickly and AEC became the first volume manufacturer to offer its own diesel, when it launched the 95 bhp A155 engine, with Acro combustion chamber, soon after the Leeds Crossley entered service. AEC had, in fact, run an earlier Acro-influenced diesel in a 104-seat double-deck staff bus for three months from December 1928, but the fast-revving A155 was a superior product and, unlike the Gardner range, it was designed from the start for automotive use.

London General put the first three diesel-engined Regents in service between Golders Green and Pinner in December 1930, and they were joined by nine similarly-powered Renowns three months later. Other operators, including Hull, Walsall, Glasgow, Halifax and Birmingham, took early AEC diesels, but additional research, involving Sussex consulting engineers Ricardo, resulted in the appearance of an improved diesel from September 1931 and from then the AEC diesel took off. Crossley pitched in with their own 86.8 bhp engine in December 1930 and, helped in particular by orders from Manchester and Rochdale which favoured the locally-built combination of Crossley chassis, body and engine, they enjoyed a volume of business which was never to return their way. Diesel Condor sales had topped 150 by the end of 1932, but although an improved 100 bhp Ricardo-type engine—the VR6—was introduced the following year, Crossley's engines soon lagged behind and the seeds of later disaster were sown. Gardner found themselves in the unusual position of finding that their engines were proving increasingly popular in an application which had never been considered by the makers. Yet they showed commendable business sense in developing a lighter, more compact and more powerful bus engine, the LW-range, in 1931. By way of comparison, the 102 bhp 6LW weighed the same as the 4L2. This proved to be a masterstroke and the 5LW in particular, which met most operators' performance requirements and fitted into the space occupied by many six-cylinder petrol engines, became a very popular unit. Daimler's COG5, bought in large numbers by municipalities like Birmingham, had this engine and first appeared at the 1933 Commercial Motor Show. Bristol standardised on the 5LW for diesel versions of its G-type double-decker and J-type single-decker from 1933, and Guy launched its 6LW-engined Arab double-decker the same year, designed from the outset as a diesel bus.

Gardner engines were used extensively by operators who re-equipped petrol-engined vehicles in their fleets, and they also found their way into some low-volume models. In this latter category were 4LW and 6LW-engined Fodens produced from 1933, six 6LW-engined Gloster-Gardner coaches built in 1933 for Red and White by the Gloucester Railway Carriage and Wagon Company, and the 5LW-engined GNR-Gardner single-deckers built from 1937 by Ireland's Great Northern Railway. Irish operators were compelled to buy buses assembled in the country but, while Great Southern and Dublin United bought British vehicles in kit form, GNR went a stage further and designed its own bus around the 5LW, Kirkstall axles, Meadows gearbox, Hardy-Spicer propshaft and CAV-Bosch lighting and fuel equipment. Forty were built in 1937/38 and production continued until 1952.

Although Leyland had made steady advances in the bus market and had produced a prototype 78 bhp diesel engine for the 1931 Commercial Motor Show, they waited until 1933 before putting their 8.1-litre into production. An 8.6-litre 93 bhp engine succeeded it by the end of the year. The delay paid off, for while Crossley suffered from being in with a crude product which they failed to improve, Leyland's superior research, sales and production resources were to sweep them into a very strong position just when the industry was ready to buy diesels in quantity. Albion launched their own diesel in 1933 and also offered Gardner options. Both Dennis and Midland Red had their own power units a year later. There also were diesels available from Tangye, Dorman, Beardmore and Armstrong Saurer (Swiss Saurer designs built in Newcastle-upon-Tyne by Armstrong Whitworth), and the lighter end of the market, which tended to stick longest with petrol power, got its diesels from Perkins, which started business in 1932, and Gardner, which introduced the 57 bhp 4LK in 1935. AEC launched its four-cylinder diesel in 1933.

Municipal operators showed great faith in diesels and, encouraged by earlier figures which showed operating costs of about a quarter of those for petrol-engined buses, had converted 27 per cent of their combined fleets by 1935. By 1937, Leyland reported that 85 per cent of its buses were being supplied with diesels and, between 1937 and 1938, the number of diesel buses in Britain rose from 13,000 to over 17,000, while the population of petrol buses fell from 36,000 to 33,000. Not a bad advance from March 1930.

The tax advantage of diesel fuel did not last long. A 1d (½p) tax was introduced in 1933 and this went up to 8d (3½p) in 1935. Despite howls of anguish from the industry, the 1935 increase added only about ½d (0.25p) to operating costs per mile, and the diesel had established itself so firmly by then that it maintained its supremacy. That supremacy had its roots in places like Manchester, which standardised on diesels from 1932, and Birmingham which followed suit two years later. Glasgow showed caution to begin with, but after experimenting with AEC, Leyland, Beardmore and Gardner engines, put its faith in the first two makes and had its entire fleet re-equipped by 1938. It was the first municipality to do this and turned a bus deficit of £10,000 into a £639 surplus as a result.

Red and White claims the distinction for having the first all-diesel fleet. After fitting a Gardner 5LW and a 4LW into Albions in 1931 (an associate company was an agent for both makes), they embarked on a conversion programme on their 400-vehicle fleet from 1933 to 1935. Buses got 4LWs, express buses 5LWs, and coaches 6LWs, and not only Albions, but Leylands and AECs were treated.

SMT had begun to dabble with diesels by 1932, when their Midland company (later part of Western SMT) stole some of the limelight at the opening of Victoria Coach Station with the introduction of diesel-engined AEC Regals on the 410-mile Glasgow route. In 1933/34, they ordered 550 Leyland 8.6-litre engines for a massive re-equipment programme, and gave themselves the world's largest diesel fleet at the time.

By the end of 1933, London Transport had 179 diesel buses, most of them AEC-engined Regents and Renowns. The Hanwell garage was converted completely and Hammersmith was 87 per cent diesel. By 1935, the total had risen to 850, and petrol engines were no longer being bought.

A diminishing number of operators clung to petrol engines, at least for some of their orders. Eastbourne avoided diesels until 1946, despite cost savings which even it acknowledged, and Ireland's Great Southern Railways were still buying petrol Leylands in 1937, when the SMT-associated Dublin United had standardised on diesel. Even Ribble, on Leyland's doorstep and one of the country's largest operators, had only 75 diesels (all Titan double-deckers) in their 1937 fleet of over 1,000 buses. And Wallasey, which had forsaken petrol earlier in the 1930s, bought seven petrol Titans in 1938 when Leyland introduced a new range of engines, primarily for fire appliances. However, they were exceptions and Halifax Corporation took the diesel into its next stage of development in 1939 when they increased the power of a 130 bhp 8.8-litre AEC Regent to 170 bhp. Long, steep hills presented the undertaking with peculiar operating requirements and, in order to provide as fast a service as possible, they fitted the Regent with a Centric supercharger which boosted the engine. This astonishingly powerful bus still managed 6.5 mpg in Halifax's arduous conditions, against 3.6 mpg for some 155 bhp petrol buses, and promised to save £2,000 a year.

The rapid rise of the diesel snuffed out some less well advanced improvements on the petrol engine before they got beyond the experimental stage. Most smacked a little too closely of the ideas of W. Heath Robinson, but, in the years before the diesel established itself, they represented an alternative, and cheaper, way ahead for operators who did not want to re-engine their fleets. Edinburgh Corporation and the Belfast Omnibus Company turned to their city gas works betwen 1931 and 1933, and had buses fuelled by coal tar, a by-product of gas production. In 1933, a good year for alternative fuel, South Midland had a Gilford coach on their Oxford—London run converted to burn a mixture of creosote and petrol, and London General was carrying out a similar experiment with five buses. The South Midland coach used 28 gallons of creosote and 3.5 gallons of petrol where it would normally have used 30 gallons of petrol, but the creosote cost only 7d (3½p) a gallon. And in a similar vein, Cambridge-based Varsity Express, which sold out to Thomas Tilling later the same year, converted AEC Regal and Leyland Tiger coaches to burn a mixture of vaporising oil and petrol, using a device invented by company chairman H.A. Harvey and known as Harvey's Paraffin Attachment.

More serious experiments were carried out with compressed town gas, carried in cylinders under the bus. Birmingham converted a 32-seat Guy in time for the February 1933 British Industries Fair, and its seven 350 cu ft cylinders gave it a 65-mile range. Northern General put a converted 37-seat SOS into service around the same time in the Newcastle area, and claimed a 70-mile range for it. It was still in service in 1939. Similar experiments were carried out briefly by Rotherham, Lincoln and Chesterfield and, in May 1936, Wallasey put a gas-powered double-decker on its New Ferry route. Initially, it only had a 12-mile range, although this was improved, but in the absence of suitable equipment, the project was abandoned after a year. Gas buses also carried a weight penalty (Rotherham reckoned this to equal about three passengers), but their rejection in Britain contrasted with Germany where, by 1937, the Nazi Government had 400 buses, 23 of them in Berlin, powered by gas as part of a programme of fuel self-sufficiency. Around 40 public gas stations were in use in Germany by 1938. The alternative to compressed gas was producer gas, which was created by burning coal, wood or turf on the vehicle. France encouraged producer gas development throughout the 1930s as a hedge against fuel crises and, as war became more likely, interest grew in Britain. But the Coal Utilisation Council complained in December 1938 that, while Britain had 23 producer gas vehicles (two of them buses), France had over 4,000, Sweden 70, Italy 1,500 and Russia was planning to have 80,000 by 1940.

Britain's first bus was the Gilford HSG, built in 1937 at the former Gilford works in London around a 1935 CF176 chassis. The HSG part of the name came from High Speed Gas (Great Britain) Ltd, who had bought Gilford's premises, and their producer gas expertise was put to use in converting the 7.4-litre AEC petrol engine to 8.1 litres to develop 85 bhp, and to fit an anthracite burner at the rear. The bus was bought by Highland Transport, who at one time entertained notions of converting it to run on readily-available peat, and later charcoal. Highland chairman Sir Alexander MacEwen joined forces with the Duke of Montrose to form the British Gazogenes Company, which was to market the French Gohin Poulenc producer gas system in Britain, and such equipment was specified by Highland for a gas-powered Albion Valkyrie ordered in 1939.

The Gilford proved cheap to operate on Highland's comparatively gentle Inverness—Dornoch route, where it returned figures of 0.65d per mile against 1d (½p) for diesel buses and 1.9d for petrol buses; but a 23-day trial with Glasgow Corporation during the 1938 Empire Exhibition revealed its sluggish performance and unsuitability for city work. Undeterred, HSG built a second vehicle, the Sentinel-HSG, in time for the 1938 Scottish Motor Show. Unlike horizontally-engined Sentinel-HSG lorries built at the same time in conjunction with the Shrewsbury steam wagon builder, the 90 bhp bus had a conventional front engine and rear burner. It was demonstrated in Merthyr Tydfil in early 1939, and South Wales Transport tried it on the hilly Swansea-Caswell Bay route later the same year.

World events kindled more interest from such operators as West Yorkshire, Chesterfield and Eastern Counties, who adapted older vehicles in 1939, but in the absence of Government direction, this was a slow and reluctant display of interest.

By 1930, the pressure to improve gearbox design also was building up. London General had remarked a year earlier that 'the clutch is still an almost uncivilised device', for although the conventional manual gearbox was simple to maintain, it produced slow gearchanges and required a degree of skill from the driver. With a growing number of tram drivers being retrained as busmen, that last point was very important. Daimler broke with tradition when they launched their CH6 range in October 1930. In place of the preceding CG6's sliding mesh gearbox and single-plate clutch was a Wilson pre-selective gearbox and fluid flywheel which only required the driver to select the correct gear, then engage it by depressing

A four-cylinder diesel-engined AEC Regal 4, new in 1934 to Provincial's Gosport and Fareham fleet. The 32-seat body was built by Thomas Harrington, at Hove (J.F. Higham).

a gear pedal. The transmission, which hitherto had been fitted to cars, added £100 to the chassis price, but its reduced maintenance costs, faster gear-changes and ease of operation made it a very worthwhile proposition, particularly for municipal undertakings. General took three of the earliest CH6s in December 1930, purely to evaluate the gearbox and, after fitting similar units to three of their AECs in 1931, prompted AEC to start offering Daimler-built Wilson gearboxes in all of their models from 1932. From 1934, when the preselective principle was well-established, AEC manufactured their own units, most of them going to London, which had 1,700 by 1937.

Leyland went a step further and developed a semi-automatic torque converter transmission on Lysholm-Smith patents, which was first displayed around the time of the 1931 Commercial Motor Show on a Tiger 35-seater, and which was offered on Tiger, Titan, Titanic and Lion models and diesel railcars two years later. Apart from neutral and reverse, the driver needed only to select two positions on these 'gearless' buses—converter from rest to about 20 mph and direct thereafter. There was no gear pedal. The torque converter system worked best in hilly areas, where its acceleration was superior, and Sheffield Corporation took advantage of it from 1932, when a Titan TD2c demonstrator entered service. Sheffield maintained its pioneering tradition by becoming the first operator in the country to run an all-torque converter route on March 25 1934 when ten Titans took over the No 61 Nether Edge service. The city eventually bought 167 torque converter Leylands, and had the distinction of taking the 2,000th gearbox in 1938. West Riding, which had 170 gearless Leylands by 1937, ran the world's largest fleet of the type. There was a fuel penalty with the torque converter, and this, together with its inferior behaviour in snow and ice, reduced its attractiveness to operators, few of whom looked upon it with as much favour as the Wilson boxes in Daimlers and AECs.

Others who tried to muscle in on the modern gearbox did not get so far. London General tried two German Maybach five-speed pre-selective units in 1932, a Cotal pre-selector appeared in a Southampton Guy Arab at the 1935 Show, and a Freeborn Automatic Gear four-speed torque converter was fitted to a Manchester Crossley Mancunian at the same Show.

The quietest revolution of the period was the switch away from using wood in the construction of many bodies—especially double-deckers—from 1931, when Metropolitan-Cammell built their first production all-metal bodies, among them 25 on Dennis Lance double-deckers for London General subsidiary Overground. By the following year, they had pooled resources with Weymann of Addlestone and had formed Metro-Cammell Weymann which controlled the design, development and sale of all-metal bodies produced by the two companies. When Crossley started building all-metal bodies in 1933, they used MCW shells. Burlingham and Leyland built their first metal bodies in 1932 and Park Royal started the following year.

In tandem, the introduction of diesel engines, all-metal bodies and, where used, pre-selective or torque converter transmissions helped consolidate the gains being made by the bus. For the first time, operators found they could keep their vehicles for at least ten years without rebuilding them drastically, and the resultant savings in maintenance costs increased profit margins to levels undreamt of before. In a climate in which the tram and rural railway already had the odds stacked against them, these technical advances tipped the balance a little further.

Left *Dignitaries stand back as the pioneering Midland Bus Services diesel-engined AEC Regal leaves Victoria Coach Station in March 1932 on its first London–Glasgow run* (National Bus Company).

Above *Manchester Corporation's tramcar works built its own bodywork on this 1932 Crossley Condor with Crossley Type 1 diesel. The bus was rebodied in 1937 and remained in service until 1946* (Greater Manchester Transport Museum Society).

Above right *SMT associations ensured Dublin United's specification of diesel engines in the large fleet of Leyland Titans bought for tram replacement between 1937 and 1940. This is a 1939 TD5 with Leyland body assembled by the operator* (Cyril McIntyre collection).

Right *Sheffield pioneered diesel engines and torque converter transmission. This 1933 Leyland Titan TD3c with Craven body fell between two stools, having torque converter, but petrol engine* (Leyland Vehicles).

Above *Posed against a background of Stirling Castle, this is a 1936 Leyland Cheetah LZ2 with Alexander body for the diesel-minded SMT company* (Robert Grieves collection).

Below *Another Gardner 5LW-engined bus was this Albion Valkyrie PW141, supplied to Hebble in 1937, and fitted with a 35-seat Roe body* (J.F. Higham).

Above *A 1937 Daimler COG5 with Willowbrook bodywork for Luton Corporation at that year's Commercial Motor Show in Earls Court, London* (Alan Millar collection).

Below *Tilling's Brighton, Hove and District fleet included this Gardner 5LW-powered 1936 Bristol GO5G with Tilling bodywork* (W.J. Haynes).

Above *Red and White, which had an associate company dealing in Gardner engines and Albion chassis, converted its entire fleet to diesel power by 1935. This is a Gardner 6LW-engined Albion Valiant PV71, with 32-seat Gloster coach body, new that year* (J.F. Higham).

Left *One of the three Daimler CH6 double-deckers which London General bought in 1931 to evaluate pre-selective gearboxes. It standardised on the gearbox, but sold the Daimler chassis in 1935* (J.F. Higham).

Above right *Glasgow's all-diesel fleet included 50 Cowieson-bodied gearless Leyland Titan TD4c double-deckers delivered in 1935. This one was photographed outside the City Chambers in November 1938* (Leyland Vehicles).

Right *A Northern General AEC Regal 0662 with 34-seat Brush body to British Electrical Federation standards. This vehicle was unusual in being painted mainly red, and it was destroyed by fire in 1942* (Chris Warn collection).

8
MERRYLEE
386
HS 9079
CGB 121
YS 2 32

2
NEWCASTLE
STANLEY
TANTOBIE
DUPLICATE
MARLBOROUGH CRESCENT
744
NORTHERN
CN 7959

NATIONAL PROVINCIAL BANK
MEUX'S Famous STO
53
MARGATE
CANADA CALLING BRITAIN
BUY CANADIAN PRODUCE
CKP 878

Inset *An Isle of Thanet Electric Supply Company 1936 Daimler COG5 with Weymann body. It was photographed after East Kent bought the company in March 1937* (D.W.K. Jones).

Background photograph *Although a traditional Daimler customer, Birmingham bought large numbers of Leyland Titan gearless double-deckers in the late 1930s. This Leyland-bodied TD4c, new in 1937, was photographed the following year* (Leyland Vehicles).

Top *The Gilford-HSG producer gas bus which Highland Transport bought in 1937. It was photographed during its 23-day trials on a Glasgow Corporation cross-city route* (Robert Grieves collection).

Above *Fodens built around 11 Gardner 6LW-engined chassis in 1933-5, including this service bus for the Green Bus Service, at Rugeley, in Staffordshire* (George F.T. Waugh collection).

Top *A 1931 Daimler CH6 with Middlesbrough Corporation seen at Grove Hill when new. Its unpainted body had seats for 52 passengers. The bus was scrapped in 1938* (Cleveland Transit, Middlesbrough).

Above *Representing the advanced thinking of the time, this South Shields Corporation Daimler COG5 was fitted with a 55-seat forward-entrance Weymann all-metal body* (Robert C. Davis collection).

NICE TRY, SHAME ABOUT THE SALES

The developments in bus design described in the last chapter may have transformed the industry, but where were the bus and coach equivalents of Sir Malcolm Campbell's *Bluebird*, Gresley's A4 Pacific steam locomotives, or the *Daily Express* buildings—the bold advances which owed less to what went before? They were built and, although some stalled at the starting gate, they nonetheless made their mark.

Gilford, who had built only one double-decker before, stormed into the 1931 Commercial Motor Show at London's Olympia with what must rank as the quintessential flop, a truly advanced double-decker which nobody was prepared to buy. This bus had just about everything. There was no chassis frame, but the 56-seat body was a strong, steel-framed structure built to resemble a box. It followed a German lead by having front-wheel drive—something never done since on a British bus—and was exhibited with a partially completed six-cylinder, 12-piston two-stroke Junkers diesel, and a constant mesh gearbox which protruded 4 ft into the lower saloon. And it had independent pneumatic suspension, using Glasgow-built, but American-designed Gruss air springs, similar to those fitted as standard to the front of Gilford single-deckers. The combination of chassisless construction and front-wheel drive meant there was no running gear between the axles and, apart from simplifying maintenance, this made the Gilford one of the lowest double-deckers ever built. When laden, its floor was 13⅜ in from the ground, and its 12 ft 11 in overall height, with flat floors on both decks, was better than most lowbridge double-deckers which had a sunken gangway along the offside of the top deck.

Although the Gilford was undisputed star of the 1931 show, and Wycombe carried off the novel features award for the body construction method and height, its story ended soon after. Plans to have the German Junkers diesel assembled in Britain got nowhere, and the double-decker and a 7 ft 10 in high single-deck testbed were tested instead with a Meadows petrol engine. It was rebuilt in 1932 as a trolleybus, using Electric Construction Company equipment, and saw service in Wolverhampton for the last six weeks of 1932. But both buses, whose very high development costs contributed towards Gilford's eventual bankruptcy, were scrapped a year later when the company moved out of its High Wycombe factory to occupy smaller premises in West London. It is said they only realised £7-10-0d (£7.50) scrap value.

Gilford made one last, and no more successful, venture into double-deckers in 1932/33, when it built a pair of conventionally-engineered Zeus models. The model name represented an attempt to topple Leyland's Titan from its throne, but the established Greek god stayed on top and no more Zeus models were made.

If Gilford were small manufacturers with neither the customers nor the resources to support their revolutionary design, AEC, with a big share of the London, municipal and company markets, were in a very different position. Yet its side-engined Q-type attracted little over 300 orders between 1932 and 1937, and gained few repeat orders. The Q-type was influenced by American practice, and was intended as a double-decker which, AEC hoped, would appeal to the forward-thinking London combine. It was designed to have an entrance ahead of the front axle, and had a gearbox and slightly inclined petrol or diesel engine (with minimal intrusion of the passenger area) mounted directly behind the offside front wheel, and beneath the stair case. The propshaft ran down the outside of the chassis frame to a differential just to the inside of the single offside rear wheel. A crash gearbox was fitted in the prototype, but all other models had pre-selective gearboxes.

London General took the prototype, a 35-seat single-decker, and Birmingham Corporation borrowed the first double-decker, a 60-seater, early in 1933. Sales to inquisitive municipal operators like Hull, Bolton, Birkenhead and Wallasey, helped double-deck sales stay ahead of single-deckers at first, and five trolleybuses, three for Australia, followed in 1934. But London Transport's singular lack of enthusiasm for the front-entrance layout on double-deckers—it bought only two along with two central-entrance models—meant that only 23 four-wheel double-deckers were made. London placed more faith in the Q-type as a single-decker, and its orders for 230 buses and coaches kept the model going until 1937. It also bought one last double-decker, a unique six-wheeler with electrically-operated gearbox, in 1936, and had it fitted with a 51-seat coach body for Green Line duties. But by then, London Transport and Leyland were working on other engine positions for single-deckers.

A small British company, Quest 80, revived the design and its name in 1980 when it built a side-engined single-decker for South Africa. There are plans to mass produce them in that Republic where the AEC did gain some favour, but this time with locally-built Atlantis engines.

The Q-type was considered, but rejected, by Northern General, which needed high capacity single-deckers for its services on Tyneside. Like Midland Red, with which it had close ties, it preferred to use single-deckers wherever possible, and this was reinforced by a large number of low bridges on some of its busiest routes. Consequently, out of 400 buses operated in 1933, only 13 were double-deckers. As the Q-type's engine took up too much space on a single-decker—the best seating capacity achieved was 39—Northern took the bull by the horns and designed its own bus. A prototype 30 ft long SE6 six-wheeler bus was built in 1933, and fitted with a six-cylinder side-valve Hercules WXRT petrol engine imported from America, a four-speed Fuller gearbox and Borg and Beck clutch. The third axle was a trailing one, fitted to meet Construction and Use regulations for a 30 ft bus. It was fitted with a 45-seat Short Brothers body and entered service in August 1933.

For production, a set-back front axle, giving an entrance beside the driver and an engine position nearer the rear wheels, were adopted. Sixty-seven production models, 31 of them built in 1935 by AEC, entered service between 1934 and 1939. Eight were built as touring coaches and 26 were four-wheel 40-seaters, designated SE4. The 25 production SE4s were fitted with AEC diesels which were inclined to a greater degree than on the Q-type. AEC arrived at a cheaper solution to Northern's problems in 1939 when it built special Regal single-deckers with shortened cabs and room for 38 seats. Why Northern didn't do that from the outset, even with a six-wheeler, is a mystery.

Another north-eastern operator, Venture Bus Services and Reed Brothers, of Consett, was one of the early customers for another high-capacity single-decker, the Maudslay SF40. Although it had a vertical front engine and radiator, the SF40 shared the SE4's set-back front axle and 40-seat passenger capacity, and around 100 were built by the Coventry company between 1935 and 1939. It was available with Maudslay petrol engine or Gardner 4LW and 5LW diesel engines, and from 1937 was marketed as the Magna. Most bodies were built by Willowbrook, but four 32-seat Duple-bodied Magna luxury coaches were bought by Neath and Cardiff in 1939 for their express services.

Midland Red took innovation forward by another step in 1935, when they placed Britain's first rear-engined bus in service on their Birmingham—Langley route. Three 40-seat buses and one 32-seat coach, all designated RECs and designed by company chief engineer L.G. Wyndham-Shire, were built in 1935/36 at the company's Carlyle works. They had petrol engines mounted transversely behind the rear axle, twin radiators, low floors and one bus and the coach originally had Daimler fluid flywheels and Cotal electro-magnetically operated gearboxes with two-pedal control. Although they were reputed to be smooth and quiet in service, no more were built, but they were reconstructed during the Second World War with underfloor engines under the guidance of Donald Sinclair, who had played a major part in developing Northern General's SE4 and SE6 designs.

Operators had to wait until 1937, and the first Earls Court Commercial Motor Show, for Britain's first horizontal underfloor-engined bus to appear. This was Tilling Stevens' Successor, another six-wheeler, powered by an eight-cylinder horizontally-opposed 95 bhp diesel which was mated to a seven-speed (top speed was overdrive) Maybach pre-selective gearbox. Engine and gearbox were mounted behind the front axle and drove into the rearmost axle. There were horizontally-mounted coil springs on the four rear wheels, giving a smooth ride, but adding to the complexity of an already unproven and unconventional design. The Successor, and a similar four-wheel lorry, the Yeoman, created a similar sensation to that six years earlier, when Gilford displayed their front-wheel drive double-decker. And the similarity went further, for neither a bare chassis nor a Duple-bodied coach turned a wheel in revenue-earning service. For, like Gilford, TS no longer had large customers to rely upon, and they did not have the resources to push into setting up a speculative production run.

On the other hand, Leyland had both, and their efforts dominated the second half of the 1930s. About the only failure was a magnificent six-wheel low-floor trolleybus, the TTL, which appeared at Olympia in 1935 on GEC's stand. The 30 ft bus had a set-back front axle, two 40 hp motors which drove by separate propshafts down the outsides of the chassis frame and into the fronts of the rear bogies, and had no rear axle beams. As with the Gilford, this meant that flat floors could be fitted within a low overall height, in this case 13 ft 6 in. Massey built a rear entrance/front exit body with separate staircases. Doorvac air doors were fitted at the front. London Transport tried the TTL on its Kingston—Wimbledon route before the show, and it was demonstrated elsewhere. As with the Q-type, it was probably London's reluctance to buy a front platform double-decker which prevented such a promising model from being built in quantity.

Leyland derived much of the inspiration for design advances from North America and, in 1936, its general manager, A.A. Liardet, spent two months in the United States and Canada visiting manufacturers and operators. He found that, although the petrol engine still dominated, one-man operation had killed off the bonneted bus, and rear-engined 'pusher' and underfloor-engined 'pancake' designs, some of integral or semi-integral construction, were standard. Although Leyland had a testbed bus running with an 8.6-litre diesel mounted transversely at the rear, Liardet reasoned that the greater seating capacity of the 'pancake' designs outweighed the better engine and gearbox access of the 'pusher' buses. By early 1937, the company had imported a White 'pancake' bus from the States, and set about borrowing technology from the installation of the eight-cylinder petrol engine, before fitting it with a Leyland diesel. The result of this, and two years' collaboration with London Transport, was a 'pancake'-engined Tiger, the FEC (Flat Engine Coach), which was unveiled in October 1937. The prototype Green Line FEC was powered by a 94 bhp 8.6-litre diesel which was mounted horizontally on the offside, behind the driver (the Q-type left its mark here), and had a fluid flywheel, Wilson electro-pneumatic pre-selective gearbox built by AEC, and Clayton air brakes. The LPTB-built 34-seat body reflected the operator's aversion to front entrances and had a door behind the front axle. A vertical radiator was concealed at the front and the driver enjoyed excellent visibility from a position 18 in from the ground and within a half cab.

Another 75 LPTB-bodied Green Line coaches and 12 Park Royal-bodied private hire coaches were built in 1939 and equipped with compressed air-operated gearboxes. Like the prototype, they had unit construction bodies and chassis, built directly on to the chassis, without bottom framing. This concept, also tried on trolleybuses, increased the strength of the coaches. All but one of the Park Royal coaches were destroyed in the bombing of the Bull Yard, at Peckham, in 1940.

For those with faith in British inventiveness, 1937 was a good year, for Leyland launched their six-wheel, front-engined, front-entrance Gnu single-decker at Earls Court. Until then, six-wheelers, of which most were trolleybuses, had twin rear axles, but Leyland wanted to reduce the tyre scrub and poor cornering inherent in such designs and opted instead for a twin-steer layout. The front of the Gnu was an object lesson in economy of space, with the driving position moved further offside, the engine moved as far forward as possible, and the radiator fitted to the nearside, so that there was the maximum possible room for passengers to pass the engine. Only eight were built. The show exhibit and one other went to Alexander and were fitted with their own 40-seat bodywork, and a 1938 Duple-bodied coach joined the 62-vehicle (36 of them diesel-engined six-wheel Leylands) City Coach Company fleet on the London—Southend route.

London Transport's first FEC Tiger was fitted originally with an unusual driving cab, which gave the driver excellent visibility. It started life on the Woking—Tunbridge Wells Green Line route (D.W.K. Jones).

A cutaway drawing of the Junkers diesel installed in the Gilford front-wheel drive double-decker of 1931 (Commercial Motor).

The City coach had completed 70,000 miles by August 1 1939, when the other five Gnus joined it. They were simpler models, with conventionally-mounted radiators, no front overhang and full bulkheads behind the driver. One twin-steer Leyland trolleybus was built for London in 1939, but remained unique.

The Gnu and FEC Tiger came together in the Panda, a twin-steer horizontal mid-engined chassis, similar in layout to the 1939 Gnus and completed soon after them. The solitary example went to Alexander, who fitted it with a 45-seat central entrance body, and placed it in service in May 1941, when such advanced technology was one of the industry's lowest priorities.

Leyland's Kingston-on-Thames factory continued to persevere with rear-engined designs for the Cub range, which had insufficient space beneath the floor for a horizontal engine. They did some useful work on the possibilities of transverse and longitudinal engines, even of twin engines, before building a prototype 20-seater REC (Rear Engine Cub) for London Transport in 1938. It had a longitudinal vertical 4.7-litre diesel, constant mesh gearbox, and radiator, all mounted behind the rear axle. Its LPTB body was a scaled-down version of the FEC Tiger design, but was designed for one-man operation on London's quieter routes. Another 59 were ordered for delivery in 1939, but only 48 arrived, owing to the outbreak of war.

The very fact that British manufacturers were able to poach foreign designs for these advanced vehicles shows that they were by no means new ideas. So why did Britain, which had a healthy bus and coach industry, lag behind? Much of the blame must lie in the detail of the 1930 Act. The limit on the size of one-man operated buses snuffed out an area in which front entrance designs would have proved attractive. Similarly, had two-axle 30 ft long buses been authorised, underfloor-engined 45-seaters would have made a more economical alternative to the 56-seat double-decker. And the removal of competition after 1931 also swept away some of the one-upmanship which might have encouraged coach operators, in particular, to run progressively more modern vehicles. Nor did Britain's road network help. Without such fast roads as Nazi Germany's autobahns, of which 3,395 km were built by 1939, British operators did not need high-powered buses, and were unlikely to buy them even if they were available. While visitors to the 1935 Berlin motor show could marvel at a streamlined front- and rear-engined Büssing-NAG 280 bhp coach capable of 75 mph, and Americans enjoyed State highway travel throughout the 1930s in 35 ft long 70 mph coaches, the British operator, restricted to 30 mph on single-carriageway roads, was more than satisfied with 95 bhp.

Top *One of the first production SE6s, with set back front axle and 44-seat Short Brothers body. It was new in 1934* (Michael Heard collection).

Above *Northern General's prototype SE6 single-decker with the side flap lifted to reveal its Hercules petrol engine* (Michael Heard collection).

Left *A post-war view of one of the five Duple-bodied Gnu TEC2 coaches which City placed in service in August 1939 on its London—Southend service. In many respects, they were twin-steer Tigers* (W.J. Haynes).

Top *Wallasey Corporation bought two central-entrance Roe-bodied Q-types in 1934. Note the 'Corporation Motors' fleetname used by the Wirral municipalities* (R.L. Wilson collection).

Above *The Leyland Panda underfloor-engined chassis built for Alexander in 1939, and bodied two years later. This photograph was taken in March 1940, when Leyland had begun to build military equipment* (Leyland Vehicles).

Right *The prototype AEC Q-type in service with London Transport's country department. The engine was fitted behind the front axle. A tramcar lifeguard was fitted at the front as a safety measure* (D.W.K. Jones).

Above *Alexander bought two of the three Leyland Gnu TEP1 six-wheelers. This one was a bus, the other a coach* (Leyland Vehicles).

Left *A rear view of one of London Transport's rear-engined Leyland Cub one-man buses, taken in September 1939 after blackout markings had been applied* (London Transport).

Below *Two of the Maudslay SF40 front-engined single-deckers run by Venture, of Consett. These 1935 examples had Willowbrook 40-seat bodies and were run by the subsidiary Yellow Bus Service, of High Spen, until 1938* (Chris Warn collection).

One of the two forward-entrance Q-type double-deckers bought by London Transport on service from Harrow Weald garage (London Transport).

A dozen of London Transport's FEC Tigers were built for private hire and sightseeing tours, and had sunshine roofs incorporated in their Park Royal bodies. Only this one was to survive the 1939-45 war (London Transport).

So far ahead of its time, that it failed to go into production, the Leyland TTL trolleybus had the lines of buses being built 25 years later. It was photographed on trial in February 1935 (Leyland Vehicles).

THE LURE OF THE SKIES

An entrepreneur who has developed a business from nothing into a thriving enterprise soon becomes bored if faced with no new challenges. By 1931, the Road Traffic Act and the relentless growth of the combine companies effectively killed off the chances for further expansion by the enterprising pioneers of the bus and coach industry. But, fortified in many cases by cash payments from the new shareholders in their businesses, they looked elsewhere to develop their skills and several took to the skies.

Air transport was a logical step for busmen. It was as new and undeveloped in 1930 as the motor-bus industry had been when these pioneers had entered it; it involved the use of internal combustion engined equipment; and it needed new blood to break it out of the staid, colonial mould of Imperial Airways, the British Government's subsidised international airline. There also was such faith in air transport, somewhat misplaced as it turned out, that many believed it could take over the roles performed by many road and rail vehicles of the time. One of the earliest air transport ventures by busmen was launched in the summer of 1930 when National Coachways and Glenton Friars offered through bookings by coach and seaplane from Scotland, Newcastle and London to Calais via Dover. In July 1932 Solent Coaches, of Portsmouth, began a London—Isle of Wight service five times each day, with passengers transferring to an eight-seat Westland Wessex aircraft for the Portsmouth—Ryde section.

While these ventures were fairly safe investments for the coach operators concerned, it was the full-blooded air transport involvement of Edward Hillman, Scottish Motor Traction, John Sword, George Nicholson, and W.L. Thurgood, and other operators' associations with regular short-haul air services which justifies this chapter.

Hillman had only started his coach business in December 1928, but after three years had 107 Gilfords in service between London, its eastern suburbs and the Essex and East Anglian resorts. He started Hillman Airways in December 1931, with the first of three two-seater De Havilland Puss Moths (the third was named *Gilford* after his faithful coaches), and offered charter and air taxi flights for 3d (1.25p) per passenger per mile from Maylands Aerodrome, near Romford. Such was Hillman's showmanship, that in 1932 he flew a Puss Moth from Romford to AEC's works at Southall to place an order for a six-wheel Renown coach for his Romford—Clacton service. He claimed this was the first time an aeroplane had been used for such a purpose and, ironically, the coach—Hillman's only non-Gilford—ended its life the victim of an aircraft, when London Transport's Bull Yard, Peckham, premises were bombed in October 1940. The Hillman philosophy was similar to that of Sir Freddie Laker half a century later. He wanted air transport to be available to the ordinary man, his wife and family, and that meant a 'no frills' service, with pilots being paid comparatively low wages and being accorded the same status as his coach drivers. He was blessed—for much of the time—with a loyal and enthusiastic workforce and, by a labour market which worked in the employer's favour. When 200 of his bus drivers and conductors went on unofficial strike in July 1933, Hillman sacked the lot and had them replaced by unemployed staff.

Hillman started a Romford—Clacton service in April 1932, with a coach/air fare from London of 15/- (75p) single, or 21/- (£1.05) day return, and reported a £670 loss at the end of the first season. But he had carried 18,000 passengers (compared with 9 million on his coaches), and had bigger plans for the next year. A Margate service was added to the Clacton route, but thanks to the arrival of six six-seater De Havilland Dragons, he was able to tap a much bigger market by starting a twice-daily service to Paris for £3-10-0d (£3.50) single, £5-10-0d (£5.50) return, or £4-15-0d (£4.75) weekend return, and this was extended in the summer to Vichy for

£7-10-0d (£7.50) single. By 1934, the air services were starting to show a profit and were strengthened by the arrival of eight-seat Dragon Rapides and the move to a new base, Essex Airport, at Stapleford Abbotts, 5½ miles from Maylands. The new 180-acre site was a big improvement on the spartan premises used before, and had its own wireless, customs, passport and restaurant facilities. Midland and Scottish Air Ferries' London—Belfast service was taken over in July 1934 and extended to Glasgow on December 1 when Hillman won an air mail contract. This was the first time that United Kingdom mail went by air without any special fee or labelling.

Apart from two 14-seat Gilford AS6s used between London and Essex Airport, all of Hillman's coaches were taken over by the London Passenger Transport Board and Eastern National during 1934 and, on December 12, Hillman Airways Ltd was registered as a public company, with Edward Hillman as managing director. Sadly, only 19 days later, its founder was dead, aged only 45. Despite the inevitable traumas which followed, including the quick departure of Hillman's 22-year-old son following his 'complete disagreement over future policy', the company prospered. Wages and operating standards were tightened up, staff were issued with uniforms and three 10-12-seat DH86 aircraft were bought for the Paris service. A Hull—Manchester—Liverpool, and London—Le Zoute—Brussels service started in June 1935. Thanet—Le Zoute trips were added the following month when a new airport opened to serve Margate and Ramsgate, and plans were in hand to move from Essex to Gatwick Airport when the company was taken over by British Airways in December 1935.

Scotland's mountainous terrain and numerous sea crossings offered possibilities which several pioneering airmen were quick to exploit. Scottish Motor Traction set up an aviation department in July 1932 and the following year had 22 aircraft available for charters, taxi work and sightseeing tours from over 60 airfields in Scotland and the North of England. SMT's railway owners never sanctioned the company's expansion into scheduled services, and after concentrating activities on its Macmerry flying school, outside Edinburgh, SMT's aviation department was closed down in 1934. It was left to another SMT figure, John Sword, to pioneer some of Scotland's internal air services as a private venture. Sword, whose other business interests included baking, had formed Midland Bus Services in 1924 and got around £200,000 for it when SMT took control in 1929. In 1932, he was made general manager of Western SMT. He formed Midland and Scottish Air Ferries Ltd in 1933 and operated charters initially from Hooton, Cheshire, and Renfrew, near Glasgow. Scheduled services started in June 1933, with a twice-daily Renfrew—Campbeltown—Belfast route, and a three times weekly service from Renfrew to Islay via Campbeltown. The Belfast fare was £3 single, and the equivalent to Islay was £2-7-0d (£2.35). A short-lived Hooton—Liverpool—Dublin route started in August that year, with extensions on request to Cork, and the Cheshire base also was used for excursions to that year's Isle of Man TT motor cycle races and Blackpool illuminations. In all, MSAF flew 300,000 miles in its first year and carried 10,000 passengers.

In April 1934, Prime Minister Ramsay MacDonald, a personal friend of Sword, christened one of two new Avro 642 18-seaters *The Marchioness of Londonderry* after the wife of the Air Minister, and inaugurated an ambitious Romford—Belfast/Glasgow service. Aircraft ran twice daily, one from Romford via Birmingham and Liverpool to Renfrew, the other from Liverpool via the Isle of Man to Belfast. The new routes were withdrawn three months later, and Hillman, MSAF's London agent, provided a substitute Belfast route using Dragons. His flight time was 6 hours 45 minutes.

Sword cut his losses and ceased his other services at the end of September that year, saying he could not devote sufficient time to developing the airline, and it was left to Newcastle-upon-Tyne busman George Nicholson to fill the void. His Northern and Scottish Airways took over the Renfrew—Campbeltown—Islay service from December 1934, and continued the valuable air ambulance work which MSAF had begun. Northern and Scottish went on to develop internal Scottish services and was absorbed by Scottish Airways in 1937.

Ware, Hertfordshire, coachbuilder W.L. Thurgood started the People's Motor Services Ltd in 1928, but it was taken over in November 1933 by the London Passenger Transport Board. Thurgood reinvested the proceeds of the sale with commedable haste and had Jersey Airways Ltd in operation within three weeks. Its first Dragon provided a 75-minute flight from Portsmouth to Jersey for £1-12-6d (£1.62½) single, compared to the nine-hour sea crossing at £1-13-6d (£1.67½) first class and £1-1-0d (£1.05) third class single. The service was extended to London (Heston) in January 1934, with a single fare of £2-19-6d (£2.97½) for a two-hour flight and, after the first year, the company had carried 19,886 passengers in 3,912 crossings. By then, the Dragon fleet had grown to eight.

Jersey Airways graduated to four-engined DH86 Express 14-seaters, and started running to Rennes and Paris, but it did not forget its bus industry roots. As part of London Coastal Coaches' celebrations of Victoria Coach Station's third birthday, a Dragon was displayed in the station on March 14 1935.

There also were a few partnerships between major bus and coach operators and pioneer airlines which could not afford their own booking offices or ground transport. From early 1933, Red and White handled bookings for a Cardiff—Bristol service started the previous autumn by Norman Edgar Ltd, of Bristol, and ran a feeder coach service to Cardiff Airport.

East Yorkshire Motor Services provided similar facilities for North Sea Aeriel and General Transport Ltd, of Brough, when they started running a Hull—Grimsby service in July 1933, using a three-seater Blackburn Segrave. Over 1,000 passengers used the service before it was withdrawn in November 1933. Wallace Arnold acted as West Yorkshire agent for a North Eastern Airways service started between Newcastle, Leeds and London in 1935, and Westcliff-on-Sea Motor Services Ltd handled Southend bookings for an hourly Southend—Rochdale service started in 1934 by Short Brothers and Southend-on-Sea Flying Services. Others learned the lesson. The main-line railways exercised their five-year-old powers in 1934, and formed Railway Air Services which helped build up the country's internal services. But the efforts of the pioneer busmen helped develop a pre-war internal air network which did not re-emerge on a useful scale until some 30 years had passed.

Left *One of Midland and Scottish Air Ferries' Dragons at Blackpool in 1933, before taking off with a Leyland Motors party bound for the Scottish Tramways and Transport Association conference at Gleneagles. John Sword is the bowler hatted figure second from the right* (Leyland Vehicles).

Below left *Hillman's last passengers were carried to and from Central London in two Wycombe-bodied Gilford Hera 24-seaters which had a bullion compartment in the rear. New in 1935, they were taken over by British Airways, and later were absorbed into the British Overseas Airways Corporation road fleet* (D.W.K. Jones).

Above right *The AEC Renown coach which Hillman bought in 1932, after placing his order by air. The Harrington-bodied coach was taken over by London Transport in 1934, and was destroyed in a bombing raid in 1940* (P.J. Carr collection).

Right *Publicity for Northern and Scottish on a 1936 Leyland Titan in Alexander's fleet* (Robert Grieves collection).

HILLMAN'S
PRIVATE
EV 7340
0677

GO BY AIR
PHONE RENFREW 250
By NORTHERN & SCOTTISH
AIRPORT FOR GLASGOW, RENFREW
•ISLE OF MAN
•BELFAST
•ISLAY
•THE HEBRIDES
•CAMPBELTOWN
GLASGOW
PRIVATE HIRE COACHES ANY NUMBER ANY TIME
R110
W ALEXANDER & SONS LTD

APPENDICES

1. Chronology of events

1930	March	First diesel bus in service in Sheffield.
	April	Manchester converts service 53 from trams to buses.
	July	Green Line coaches start in London.
	August	Glasgow granted monopoly powers for municipal buses and trams.
	October	Daimler announces fluid flywheel/Wilson gearbox development.
	December	Herbert Morrison announces plan for ban on coaches within central London.
1931	January	Royal Commission on Transport recommends an end to tramway development. Traffic Commissioners start work. LMS Ro-Railer demonstrated.
	March	Morrison drops plans for London coach ban. London Passenger Transport Bill presented.
	April	Traffic Commissioners hold first hearings.
	May	London's first trolleybus service starts.
	July	First appeals against Traffic Commissioners' decisions lodged with Minister of Transport. Eastern Counties Omnibus Company established. Plans floated for South East Lancashire and East Cheshire Transport Board. Metro-Cammell starts production of all-metal bodies.
	August	Herbert Morrison resigns with fall of Labour Government.
	September	John Pybus (Liberal) appointed Minister of Transport. Gardner launches LW engine range.
	October	Bedford bus range announced. Gilford front-wheel drive double-decker built.
	November	Leyland exhibits prototype torque converter gearbox. Gleeson Robinson announces restrictions on coaches in London.
1932	February	Amulree Committee appointed to deal with appeals against London coach restrictions.
	March	Victoria Coach Station, London opens.
	June	Central and Western SMT companies set up.
	July	Road Transport Act, 1932 takes effect, Irish Free State.
	September	First AEC Q-type in service with London General.
1933	February	First gas bus in service, Birmingham.
	March	Pybus resigns from Parliament. Oliver Stanley (Conservative) appointed Minister of Transport.
	July	London Passenger Transport Board takes over.
	August	First Northern General SE6 enters service.
1934	January	Last GWR bus service taken over by Southern National. Road Transport Act, 1933 takes effect, Irish Free State.
	July	Associated Motorways start co-ordinated coach services through Cheltenham. Stanley becomes Labour Minister. Leslie Hore-Belisha (Liberal) becomes Transport Minister.
1935	May	Midland Red REC prototype enters service.
	July	MHCSA merged with Road Haulage Association to form Associated Road Operators.

1935 cont:	August	Northern Ireland Road Transport Board holds first meeting.
	September	Leyland TTL trolleybus demonstrated to LPTB.
	November	Gilford goes into receivership.
1936	September	Nottingham withdraws last trams.
	October	North Staffordshire Passenger Transport Board plan announced.
1937	January	North Staffordshire Bill presented.
	March	North Staffordshire Bill lost. SELEC Board plan finally dropped.
	May	LPTB central area bus strike. Hore-Belisha becomes War Secretary. Leslie Burgin (Liberal) appointed Minister of Transport. Gilford-HSG producer gas bus announced.
	September	German Road Delegation recommends motorways for Britain.
	October	Leyland Gnu and Tilling Stevens Successor announced.
	November	Leyland Tiger FEC prototype announced.
1938	January	Leyland Cub REC prototype built.
	March	Belfast trolleybus service starts.
1939	April	Burgin moves to Ministry of Supply. Euan Wallace (Conservative) appointed Minister of Transport. Brighton starts municipal bus service.
	July	LPTB places first RT double-decker in service.
	August	LPTB withdraws Green Line coaches for conversion into war ambulances.

2. Buses on British market 1930-9

Note that, in some cases, the dates of availability of chassis do not necessarily conform to dates when the vehicles were actually built, and that some double-deck models were fitted with single-deck bodies and vice versa.

Under engine position, (F) denotes a forward control vehicle, and (N) a normal control (bonneted) vehicle.

Under seating capacity, s/d denotes single-deck and d/d double-deck.

	Model	Engine position	Wheels	Seating capacity	Available	Notes
AEC	Reliance 660	Front (F)	4	35 s/d	1930/31	
	Regal 662/O662	Front (F)	4	35-39 s/d	1930-9	(a)
	Regal 4 642/O642	Front (F)	4	35 s/d	1930-9	(b)(c)
	Regal Mk II 862/O862	Front (F)	4	35 s/d	1935-9	(d)
	Regent 661/O661	Front (F)	4	56 d/d	1930-9	(a)
	Renown 663/O663	Front (F)	6	65 d/d	1930-8	(a)
	Renown 664/O664	Front (F)	6	72 d/d 39 s/d	1930-9	(a)
	Ranger 665/O665	Front (N)	4	26 s/d	1930-9	(a)
	Q-type 761/O761	Side	4	60 d/d	1932-7	(e)
	Q-type 762/O762	Side	4	39 s/d	1932-7	(e)
	Q-type O763	Side	6	51 d/d	1936	
	661T trolleybus		4	56 d/d	1930-9	
	662T trolleybus		4	35 s/d	1930-9	
	663T trolleybus		6	65 d/d	1930-6	
	664T trolleybus		6	73 d/d	1935-9	
	691T trolleybus		6	73 d/d	1933	(f)
	Q-type 761T trolleybus		4	63 d/d	1934	

(a) O-prefixed models had diesel engines (available from 1930).
(b) O-prefixed models had diesel engines (available from 1933).
(c) All Regal 4s had four-cylinder engines.
(d) O-prefixed models had diesels. Petrol option (862) available from 1937.
(e) O-prefixed models had diesel engines.
(f) Only one built (for London United Tramways).

	Model	Engine position	Wheels	Seating capacity	Available	Notes
AJS	(A.J. Stevens, Wolverhampton)					
	Pilot	Front (F/N)	4	26 s/d	1930/31	
	Commodore	Front (F)	4	32 s/d	1930/31	
Albion	PD41	Front (N)	4	16 s/d	1930/31	
	Viking PKA26/PKB26	Front (N)	4	29 s/d	1930-2	
	Viking PMA28/PMB28	Front (F)	4	32 s/d	1930-2	
	Victor PH49	Front (N)	4	20 s/d	1930-4	
	Victor PHA49	Front (N)	4	24 s/d	1934/35	
	Victor PHB49	Front (N)	4	20 s/d	1934/35	
	Victor PH111	Front (N)	4	26 s/d	1934/35	
	Victor PH114	Front (N)	4	24 s/d	1936-9	
	Victor PH115	Front (F)	4	26 s/d	1935-9	
	Victor PK114	Front (N)	4	28 s/d	1936-9	
	Victor PK115	Front (F)	4	32 s/d	1935-9	
	Valkyrie PX65	Front (F)	4	32 s/d	1930-2	
	Valkyrie PW65	Front (F)	4	36 s/d	1932-4	
	Valkyrie PW67	Front (F)	4	36 s/d	1934-6	
	Valkyrie PW69	Front (F)	4	39 s/d	1935/36	
	Valkyrie PV141	Front (F)	4	38 s/d	1936/37	
	Valkyrie PW141	Front (F)	4	40 s/d	1936/37	
	Valkyrie PW145	Front (F)	6	40 s/d	1936-9	
	Valkyrie PR145	Front (F)	6	44 s/d	1936/37	
	Valkyrie CX9	Front (F)	4	40 s/d	1937-9	
	Valkyrie CX11	Front (F)	4	38 s/d	1937-9	
	Valkyrie CX13	Front (F)	4	36 s/d	1937-9	
	Valiant PV70	Front (F)	4	36 s/d	1931-5	
	Valiant PV71	Front (F)	4	36 s/d	1935-7	
	Venturer 80	Front (F)	4	56 d/d	1933-5	
	Venturer 81	Front (F)	4	56 d/d	1935-8	
	Venturer CX19	Front (F)	4	56 d/d	1938/39	
	Valorous 85	Front (F)	6	60 d/d	1934	(a)
	(a) Only one built (as demonstrator).					
Austin		Front (N)	4	26 s/d	1939	
BAT	Cruiser	Front (N)	4	20 s/d	1930	
Bean		Front (N)	4	20 s/d	1930	
		Front (F)	4	26 s/d	1930	
	WSY	Front (F)	4	17 s/d	1930	
Bedford	WHB	Front (N)	4	14 s/d	1931-3	
	WLB	Front (N)	4	20 s/d	1931-4	
	WTL	Front (N)	4	26 s/d	1935	
	WTB	Front (N)	4	26 s/d	1936-9	
	OB	Front (N)	4	26 s/d	1939	
Berna (Swiss)	E4NOF	Front (N)	4	42 s/d	1930	
		Front (N)	6	42 s/d	1930	
Bristol	B	Front (F)	4	32 s/d	1930-3	
	C	Front (F)	6	60 d/d	1930	

	Model	Engine position	Wheels	Seating capacity	Available	Notes
	D	Front (F)	4	32 s/d	1930-3	
	E (trolleybus)		6	60 d/d	1931	(a)
	G	Front (F)	4	48 d/d	1931-7	
	H	Front (F)	4	34 s/d	1933	
	J	Front (F)	4	34 s/d	1932-7	
	K	Front (F)	4	56 d/d	1937-9	
	L	Front (F)	4	36 s/d	1937-9	
	(a) Two built (one for Doncaster; one for Pontypridd).					
Brockway (Canadian)	JC	Front (N)	4	16 s/d	1930	
	JBC	Front (N)	4	20 s/d	1930	
	SC	Front (N)	4	24 s/d	1930	
	HB	Front (N)	4	28 s/d	1930	
	HBF	Front (F)	4	32 s/d	1930	
Büssing (German)		Front (N)	4	32 s/d	1930	
Chevrolet	AC	Front (N)	4	7 s/d	1930/31	
	LQ	Front (N)	4	14 s/d	1930	
Citroen (French)	35 cwt	Front (N)	4	14 s/d	1930/31	
		Front (N)	4	20 s/d	1932/33	
Clyde	(Mackay and Jardine, Wishaw)					
	Bus	Front (N)	4	20 s/d	1930-3	
	Safety Six	Front (N)	4	26 s/d	1930-4	
Commer	Invader 6TK	Front (N)	4	20 s/d	1930-4	
	Avenger NF6	Front (F)	4	32 s/d	1930-4	
	Centaur	Front (N)	4	20 s/d	1932-5	
	Corinthian	Front (N)	4	26 s/d	1932/33	
	Centurian	Front (N)	4	20 s/d	1934/35	
	Greyhound	Front (F)	4	26 s/d	1934/35	
	PN3	Front (N)	4	20 s/d	1936-9	
	PN4	Front (N)	4	20 s/d	1936/37	
	PNF4	Front (F)	4	26 s/d	1936/37	
	PLNF5	Front (F)	4	26 s/d	1936-9	
	Superpoise	Front (N)	4	20/32 s/d	1939	
Crossley	Hawk	Front (N)	4	26 s/d	1930-3	
	Eagle	Front (F)	4	32 s/d	1930-2	
	Alpha	Front (F)	4	32 s/d	1930-9	
	Condor	Front (F)	4	52 d/d	1930-5	
	Condor six-wheel	Front (F)	6	60 d/d	1934	(a)
	Delta	Front (F/N)	4	20 s/d	1934/35	
	Mancunian	Front (F)	4	56 d/d	1934-9	
	TDD4 trolleybus		4	56 d/d	1936-9	
	TDD6 trolleybus		6	68 d/d	1936-9	
	(a) Only one built (for Manchester).					
Daimler	CF6	Front (F)	4	32 s/d 54 d/d	1930	
	CF6	Front (N)	4	32 s/d	1930	

	Model	Engine position	Wheels	Seating capacity	Available	Notes
	CG6	Front (F)	4	32 s/d 54 d/d	1930/31	
	CH6	Front (F)	4	32 s/d 54 s/d	1930-5	
	CP6	Front (F)	4	32 s/d 52 s/d	1931-7	
	COG5	Front (F)	4	56 d/d	1933-9	(a)
	COG6	Front (F)	4	56 d/d	1935-9	
	COA6	Front (F)	4	56 d/d	1934-9	(b)
	COS4	Front (F)	4	32 s/d	1935	(c)
	COT4	Front (F)	4	32 s/d	1934	(d)
	COG5/40	Front (F)	4	40 s/d	1937-9	
	COG5/60	Front (F)	4	60 d/d	1939	
	CTM4 trolleybus		4	56 d/d	1936-8	
	CTM6 trolleybus		6	60 d/d	1936-8	
	(a) Also available as 32-seat single-decker.					
	(b) AEC 7.7- or 8,8-litre engine. Supplied only to Coventry.					
	(c) Ten built for Newcastle. Fitted with Armstrong Saurer engine.					
	(d) One built for Edinburgh. Fitted with Tangye engine.					
De Dion (French)	LY	Front (N)	4	36 s/d	1934	
	LU	Front (N)	4	36 s/d	1934	
Dennis	G	Front (N)	4	19 s/d	1930/31	
	GL	Front (N)	4	20 s/d	1930-3	
	Dart	Front (N)	4	20 s/d	1930-3	
	EV	Front (F)	4	32 s/d	1930	
	FS	Front (N)	4	30 s/d	1930	
	HS	Front (F)	4	54 d/d	1930	
	HV	Front (F)	4	54 d/d	1930	
	Lance	Front (F)	4	52 d/d	1930/31	
	Lance 2	Front (F)	4	56 d/d	1931-9	
	Arrow	Front (F/N)	4	32 s/d	1930-4	
	Lancet	Front (N)	4	32 s/d	1931-6	
	Lancet	Front (F)	4	35 s/d	1932-6	
	Lancet 2	Front (F)	4	40 s/d	1935-9	
	Ace	Front (N)	4	20 s/d	1934-8	
	Ace	Front (F)	4	24 s/d	1935-7	
	Mace	Front (F)	4	26 s/d	1935-8	
	Arrow Minor	Front (N)	4	26 s/d	1937/38	
	Pike	Front (N)	4	20 s/d	1937/38	
	Falcon	Front (F)	4	26/32 s/d	1938/39	
	Falcon	Front (N)	4	20/26 s/d	1938/39	
Diamond T (Canadian)		Front (N)	4	25 s/d	1937	
Dodge	LER	Front (N)	4	20 s/d	1930	
	HEX	Front (N)	4	26 s/d	1930	
	PLB	Front (N)	4	20 s/d	1935/36	
	RB	Front (N)	4	20 s/d	1936/37	
	RBF	Front (F)	4	26 s/d	1936/37	
	SBF	Front (F)	4	26 s/d	1937-9	

	Model	Engine position	Wheels	Seating capacity	Available	Notes
Easyloader	Standard	Front (F)	4	24 s/d	1930	(a)
	(a) Adapted from dustcart chassis.					
English Electric	Trolleybus		4	35 s/d	1930	
	Trolleybus		6	60 d/d	1930	
Fargo	(Chrysler, United States)					
	Freighter	Front (N)	4	14 s/d	1930	
Federal (Canadian)	F7	Front (N)	4	20 s/d	1930	
	A6	Front (N)	4	26 s/d	1930	
	T7	Front (N)	4	32 s/d	1930	
	A6B	Front (N)	4	30 s/d	1930	
Fiat (Italian)	621RL	Front (N)	4	18 s/d	1930	
Foden		Front (F)	4	32 s/d	1933-5	
Ford/Fordson (Ford Motor Company)						
	AA	Front (N)	4	14 s/d	1930/31	
	BB	Front (N)	4	20 s/d	1933-7	(a)
	Fordalette	Front (N)	4	7 car	1931/32	(b)
	(a) Approximate dates of availability. Ceased to be advertised as a bus after 1935, but example exhibited at 1937 Commercial Motor Show. BB also offered with V8 petrol engine.					
	(b) Offered to cash on post-1930 Road Traffic Act demand for passenger vehicle capable of running at over 30 mph.					
FWD (Four Wheel Drive Motors)		Front (F)	4	20 s/d	1930	
		Front (F)	4	25 s/d	1930	(a)
	(a) Available with high or low frame.					
Garner	PAJ	Front (N)	4	20 s/d	1930/31	
	Precursor	Front (N)	4	20 s/d	1933-5	
	Progressor	Front (N)	4	20 s/d	1933-5	
Garrett	O trolleybus		4	32 s/d	1930-3	(a)
	OS trolleybus		6	60 d/d	1930-3	(a)
	(a) Last examples built 1930.					
Gilford	CP6	Front (N)	4	20 s/d	1930	
	AS6	Front (N)	4	20 s/d	1930-5	
	168SD	Front (N)	4	28 s/d	1930-5	
	168OT	Front (F)	4	32 s/d	1930-4	
	MOT	Front (F)	4	32 s/d	1931	
	Front-wheel drive	Front (F)	4	56 d/d	1931	(a)
	Hera 176S	Front (F)	4	36 s/d	1933-5	(b)
	Zeus 163D	Front (F)	4	48 d/d	1932	(c)
	Zeus T163D	Front (F)	4	56 d/d	1933	(d)
	Hermes PF140/CF140	Front (F)	4	26 s/d	1934	(e)
	PF166	Front (F)	4	28 s/d	1934	(f)
	CF176	Front (F)	4	36 s/d	1935	(g)
	(a) Only one built. Rebuilt 1932 as trolleybus.					

	Model	Engine position	Wheels	Seating capacity	Available	Notes
	(b) L176S models built for SMT group with Leyland petrol engines. D176S model with Dorman diesel engine exhibited at 1934 Scottish Motor Show.					
	(c) Only one built (demonstrator, later to Western SMT).					
	(d) Tangye diesel engine. Only one built (for Western SMT).					
	(e) None thought to have been built. PF models with Perkins Leopard diesel engine, CF with Coventry Climax petrol.					
	(f) Only three built.					
	(g) Only one built (for 1935 Commercial Motor Show). Rebuilt 1937 as Gilford-HSG producer gas bus.					
Gloster (Gloucester Railway Carriage and Wagon Company)						
	Gloster Gardner SD	Front (F)	4	35 s/d	1933/34	
	Gloster TDD trolleybus		4	54 d/d	1934	(a)
	(a) Only one built (for Southend-on-Sea).					
GMC (General Motors, United States)						
	T19	Front (N)	4	18 s/d	1930/31	
	T30	Front (N)	4	20 s/d	1930/31	
	T42	Front (N)	4	24 s/d	1930	
	T60	Front (N)	4	30 s/d	1930/31	
Great Northern Railway Company (Ireland)	GNR-Gardner	Front (F)	4	35 s/d	1937/38	(a)
	(a) Built for own use only. Production continued from 1941.					
Guy	OND	Front (N)	4	20 s/d	1930-2	
	ONDF	Front (F)	4	20 s/d	1930	
	ONDL	Front (N)	4	20 s/d	1932/33	
	Victory	Front (N)	4	20 s/d	1930-3	
	B	Front (N)	4	26 s/d	1930	
	BK	Front (N)	4	30 s/d	1930	
	FBB	Front (F)	4	35 s/d	1930	
	Conquest C	Front (N)	4	30 s/d	1930-3	
	Conquest FC	Front (F)	4	35 s/d	1930-3	
	Invincible FC	Front (F)	4	51 d/d	1930-3	
	FCX	Front (F)	6	72 d/d	1930-3	(a)
	Wolf CF	Front (N)	4	14/20 s/d	1933-9	
	Arab FD	Front (F)	4	52 d/d	1933-8	(a)
	Vixen	Front (F)	4	26 s/d	1934-9	
	BT trolleybus		4	48 d/d	1930-9	(a)
	BTX trolleybus		6	66 d/d	1930-9	(a)
	(a) Available also as single-decker.					
Halley	Talisman	Front (N)	4	24 s/d	1930/31	
	Chieftain	Front (N/F)	4	36 s/d	1930/31	
	Challenger	Front (N/F)	6	40 s/d	1930/31	
	Challenger	Front (F)	6	60 d/d	1930	
	Conqueror	Front (N/F)	4	36 s/d	1930-5	
	Clansman	Front (N/F)	4	36 s/d	1931-5	
	Neptune	Front (F)	4	51 d/d	1931-5	

	Model	Engine position	Wheels	Seating capacity	Available	Notes
International (United States)	S24	Front (N)	4	14 s/d	1930/31	
	SL34	Front (N)	4	20 s/d	1930	
	SF46	Front (N)	4	24 s/d	1930	
	A4R	Front (N)	4	26 s/d	1930-3	
	A5R	Front (N)	4	32 s/d	1930-4	
	AL3R	Front (N)	4	20 s/d	1930-3	
Karrier	Cutter	Front (N)	4	20 s/d	1930/31	
	Coaster	Front (N)	4	28 s/d	1930-3	
	Chaser Four	Front (F/N)	4	35/26 s/d	1930/31	
	Chaser Six	Front (N)	4	26 s/d	1930/31	
	Chaser Six	Front (F)	4	35 s/d	1930-4	
	Clipper	Front (F)	6	60 d/d	1930/31	
	Consort	Front (F)	6	68 d/d	1930-3	
	Monitor	Front (F)	4	50 d/d	1930	(a)
	E4 trolleybus		4	52 d/d	1931-9	
	E6 trolleybus		6	62 d/d	1930-9	
	E6A trolleybus		6	70 d/d	1935-9	
	(a) Only two built for Britain.					
Laffly (French)	LCSB	Front (N)	4	27 s/d	1930/31	
	L64 and LK64	Front (N)	4	23 s/d	1930/31	
	L65 and LK65	Front (N)	4	27 s/d	1930/31	
	LK66	Front (N)	4	32 s/d	1930/31	
Lancia (Italian)	Third Pentaiota	Front (N)	4	32 s/d	1930/31	
	Omicron	Front (F)	4	70 d/d	1930/31	
Latil (French)	BP	Front (N)	4	20 s/d	1930	
	B3G	Front (F)	4	30 s/d	1939	
	B4G	Front (F)	4	26 s/d	1939	
Leyland	Lion LT1	Front (F)	4	32 s/d	1930	
	Lion LT2	Front (F)	4	32 s/d	1930/31	
	Lion LT3	Front (F)	4	32 s/d	1931/32	
	Lion LT5	Front (F)	4	35 s/d	1932-4	
	Lion LT5A	Front (F)	4	39 s/d	1934/35	
	Lion LT5B	Front (F)	4	32 s/d	1934	(a)
	Lion LT6	Front (F)	4	32 s/d	1934/35	(b)
	Lion LT7	Front (F)	4	39 s/d	1935-7	(c)
	Lion LT8	Front (F)	4	39 s/d	1938/39	(c)
	Lion LT9	Front (F)	4	35 s/d	1938/39	(c)
	Lioness LTB1	Front (N)	4	26 s/d	1930-4	
	Tiger TS1	Front (F)	4	31 s/d	1930-2	
	Tiger TS2	Front (F)	4	31 s/d	1930-2	
	Tiger TS3	Front (F)	4	31 s/d	1930	
	Tiger TS4	Front (F)	4	32 s/d	1931-3	(c)
	Tiger TS5	Front (F)	4	32 s/d	1932	(d)
	Tiger TS6	Front (F)	4	36 s/d	1933-5	(c)
	Tiger TS6T	Front (F)	6	44 s/d	1934/35	(c)
	Tiger TS7	Front (F)	4	32 s/d	1935-7	(c)
	Tiger TS7T	Front (F)	6	44 s/d	1935-7	(c)
	Tiger TS7D	Front (F)	6	44 s/d	1935-7	(c)(e)
	Tiger TS8	Front (F)	4	32 s/d	1937-9	(c)

Model	Engine position	Wheels	Seating capacity	Available	Notes
Tiger TS8T	Front (F)	6	44 s/d	1937-9	(c)
Tiger TS8D	Front (F)	6	44 s/d	1937-9	(c)(e)
Tiger FEC	Underfloor	4	34 s/d	1937-9	(f)
Tigress LTB3	Front (N)	4	26 s/d	1934-9	
Titan TD1	Front (F)	4	51 d/d	1930/31	
Titan TD2	Front (F)	4	51 d/d	1932/33	
Titan TD3	Front (F)	4	56 d/d	1933-5	(c)
Titan TD4	Front (F)	4	56 d/d	1935-7	(c)
Titan TD5	Front (F)	4	56 d/d	1937-9	(c)
Titan TD6c	Front (F)	4	56 d/d	1938/39	(g)
Titan TD7	Front (F)	4	56 d/d	1939	(c)(h)
Titanic TT1	Front (F)	6	60 d/d	1930/31	(e)(i)
Titanic TT2	Front (F)	6	60 d/d	1932-4	(e)
Titanic TT3	Front (F)	6	60 d/d	1935-7	(e)
Titanic TT4	Front (F)	6	70 d/d	1935-7	(e)(j)
Titanic TT5c	Front (F)	6	60 d/d	1938	(e)(k)
Cub KP2/KPO2	Front (N)	4	20 s/d	1931-6	(l)
Cub KP3/KPO3	Front (N)	4	24 s/d	1931-6	(l)
Cub KP4	Front (N)	4	16 s/d	1932-4	
Cub SKP2/SKPO2	Front (F)	4	22 s/d	1932-5	(l)
Cub SKP3/SKPO3	Front (F)	4	30 s/d	1932-5	(l)
Cub KPZ1	Front (N)	4	20 s/d	1936-9	
Cub KPZ2	Front (N)	4	24 s/d	1936-9	
Cub KPZ3	Front (N)	4	20 s/d	1938/39	
Cub KPZ4	Front (N)	4	24 s/d	1938/39	
Cub SKPZ2	Front (F)	4	26 s/d	1936/37	
Cub REC	Rear	4	20 s/d	1938/39	(m)
Lion Cub SKP5/SKPO5	Front (F)	4	32 s/d	1934/35	(l)
Cheetah LZ1	Front (F)	4	37 s/d	1935/36	
Cheetah LZ1A	Front (F)	4	37 s/d	1937	
Cheetah LZ2	Front (F)	4	37 s/d	1935-7	
Cheetah LZ2A	Front (F)	4	37 s/d	1937/38	
Cheetah LZ3	Front (F)	4	26 s/d	1937/38	
Cheetah LZ4	Front (F)	4	37 s/d	1938/39	
Cheetah LZ5	Front (F)	4	26 s/d	1938/39	
Bull TQ1/TQ3	Front (F)	4	30 s/d	1930/31	(n)
Badger TA4	Front (N)	4	28 s/d	1930-6	(o)
Beaver TSC9	Front (F)	4	32 s/d	1935	(p)
Gnu TEP1	Front (F)	6	40 s/d	1937/38	(q)
Gnu TEC2	Front (F)	6	39 s/d	1939	(r)
Panda	Underfloor	6	45 s/d	1939	(s)
FA3B trolleybus		4	48 d/d	1931	(t)
TB trolleybus		4	56 d/d	1933-9	
TTB trolleybus		6	60/70 d/d	1933-9	
TTL trolleybus		6	63 d/d	1935	(u)

(a) Thirty-seven built for Alexander (fitted with six-cylinder engine).
(b) Built for Ireland and other export markets.
(c) Available with torque converter transmission and designated LT7c, etc, when so equipped.
(d) Only five built (for H.M.S. Catherwood, Belfast).
(e) Double-drive rear bogies.
(f) All 88 built for London Passenger Transport Board.
(g) All 85 built for Birmingham (fitted with torque converter).

	Model	Engine position	Wheels	Seating capacity	Available	Notes

(h) Announced October 1939.
(i) Only three built after 1929 (one demonstrator and two single-deckers for Liverpool, all in 1931).
(j) None thought to have been built.
(k) Only six built (for Doncaster), and fitted with torque converter.
(l) KPO and SKPO models fitted with diesel engine, available as option from 1934. 'O' suffix was soon dropped.
(m) All 49 built for London Transport.
(n) Adapted from lorry chassis. One of each supplied 1930 and 1931 respectively for West Monmouthshire Omnibus Board.
(o) Supplied normally as lorry.
(p) Adapted from lorry chassis. One supplied 1935 to West Monmouthshire.
(q) Three built (two for Alexander 1937, one for City Coach 1938).
(r) Only five built (for City Coach).
(s) Only one built (for Alexander).
(t) Only 12 built (for Birmingham). Converted TD1 chassis.
(u) Only one built (as demonstrator).

	Model	Engine position	Wheels	Seating capacity	Available	Notes
McCurd		Front (N)	4	26 s/d	1930	
Maudslay	Masta ML3	Front (F)	4	36 s/d	1930-6	(a)
	Montrose ML4	Front (N)	4	30 s/d	1930-4	(a)
	Marathon ML5	Front (F)	4	39 s/d	1936-9	(b)
	Meteor ML6A	Front (F)	4	36 s/d	1930-4	
	Meteor ML6B	Front (N)	4	30 s/d	1930-4	
	Mentor ML7	Front (F)	4	50 d/d	1930-4	(a)
	Magna ML7/6W	Front (F)	6	66 d/d	1930-4	
	Magna SF40	Front (F)	4	40 s/d	1935-9	(b)

(a) Model names introduced 1932.
(b) Model names introduced 1937.

	Model	Engine position	Wheels	Seating capacity	Available	Notes
Mercedes-Benz (German)	N1	Front (N)	4	18 s/d	1930/31	
	N2	Front (N)	4	32 s/d	1930/31	
	N46	Front (N)	4	24 s/d	1930/31	
	LOP	Front (F)	4	44 s/d	1938	
Minerva (Belgian)	MBR	Front (N)	4	30 s/d	1930/31	
	MBR	Front (F)	4	35 s/d	1930/31	
	HTM	Front (N)	4	28 s/d	1930/31	
	HTM	Front (F)	4	36 s/d	1930/31	
	HTMA	Front (N)	4	40 s/d	1930/31	
	HTMA	Front (F)	4	45 s/d	1930/31	
	AB2A	Front (N)	4	26 s/d	1930/31	
	2TL	Front (N)	4	18 s/d	1930/31	
	2TLA	Front (N)	4	22 s/d	1930/31	
	CR	Front (N)	4	30 s/d	1930/31	
Morris Commercial	Viceroy Y	Front (N)	4	26 s/d	1930-4	
	Dictator HB	Front (N)	4	28 s/d	1930-4	
	Dictator HF	Front (F)	4	32 s/d	1930-4	
	Imperial	Front (F)	4	56 d/d	1931-4	
	RP	Front (N)	4	20 s/d	1931-4	
	CV8 13	Front (N)	4	26 s/d	1939	

	Model	Engine position	Wheels	Seating capacity	Available	Notes
Northern General Transport	SE6	Side	6	45 s/d	1933-6	(a)
	SE4	Side	4	40 s/d	1936-9	(b)
	(a) All 42 built for NGT, 31 by AEC in 1935.					
	(b) All 26 built for NGT.					
Opel (German)		Front (N)	4	26 s/d	1938	
		Front (N)	4	32 s/d	1939	
Pagefield	(Walker Brothers, Wigan)					
	LB	Front (F)	4	36 s/d	1930/31	
	Patrician	Front (F)	4	36 s/d	1932	
Ransomes	Four-wheel trolleybus		4	56 d/d	1930-9	
	Six-wheel trolleybus		6	60 d/d	1930-9	
Renault (French)	SX	Front (N)	4	21 s/d	1930/31	
	PH	Front (N)	4	24 s/d	1930	
	RI	Front (N)	4	26 s/d	1930	
	SI	Front (N)	4	31 s/d	1930	
	OS	Front (N)	4	14 s/d	1930/31	
	T14/TD14	Front (N)	4	32 s/d	1932	(a)
	(a) TD14 fitted with four-cylinder diesel engine.					
Reo (United States)	Speedwagon FB	Front (N)	4	20 s/d	1930/31	
	GEL	Front (N)	4	26 s/d	1930/31	
	GE	Front (N)	4	25 s/d	1930-3	
Republic (United States)	FA2	Front (N)	4	28 s/d	1930/31	
Saurer (Swiss)	3BNPL	Front (N)	4	30 s/d	1930/31	
Sentinel HSG	A32P4	Front (F)	4	34 s/d	1938/39	(a)
	(a) Producer gas bus. Only one built.					
Shelvoke and Drewry	Freighter	Front (F)	4	32 s/d	1930-7	(a)
	Freighter	Rear	4	26 s/d	1938	(b)
	(a) Adapted from dustcart chassis. Engine under driver's seat.					
	(b) Only two built (for Southdown).					
Singer	Low-loading	Front (N)	4	20 s/d	1930/31	
SOS (Birmingham and Midland Motor Omnibus Company)						
	XL	Front (F)	4	30 s/d	1930	
	MM	Front (F)	4	34 s/d	1930	
	RR	Front (F)	4	30 s/d	1930	
	COD	Front (F)	4	34 s/d	1930	
	QLC	Front (N)	4	29 s/d	1930	
	SRR	Front (F)	4	30 s/d	1930	
	BRR	Front (F)	4	34 s/d	1930-4	
	IM4/IM4D/IM6	Front (F)	4	34 s/d	1930-4	(a)
	DD(RE)	Front (F)	4	52 d/d	1931-3	

	Model	Engine position	Wheels	Seating capacity	Available	Notes
	FEDD	Front (F)	4	56 d/d	1933-9	(b)
	LRR	Front (F)	4	30 s/d	1933-5	
	ON	Front (F)	4	38 s/d	1934/35	
	DON	Front (F)	4	36 s/d	1934/35	
	OLR	Front (N)	4	29 s/d	1935	
	REC	Rear	4	40 s/d	1935/36	(c)
	SON	Front (F)	4	39 s/d	1936-9	
	SLR	Front (F)	4	30 s/d	1937	
	ONC	Front (F)	4	30 s/d	1939	

(a) IM4D fitted diesel engine. IM6 fitted six-cylinder engine.
(b) Forward entrance bodies fitted to these chassis.
(c) Only four built.

	Model	Engine position	Wheels	Seating capacity	Available	Notes
Star	VB3	Front (N)	4	20 s/d	1930-2	
	VB4	Front (N)	4	26 s/d	1930-2	
Stewart (United States)		Front (N)	4	20 s/d	1930/31	
Sunbeam	Pathan SF4	Front (F)	4	32 s/d	1930-4	
	Sikh SS5	Front (F)	6	67 d/d	1930	
	Sikh SS6	Front (F)	6	60 d/d	1931-4	
	MS1 trolleybus		6	60 d/d	1932/33	
	MS2 trolleybus		6	70 d/d	1932-9	
	MF1 trolleybus		4	34 s/d	1933-9	
	MF2 trolleybus		4	56 d/d	1933-9	
	MF2A trolleybus		4	56 d/d	1933-8	(a)
	MF3 trolleybus		4	24 s/d	1935-9	
	MF3A trolleybus		4	30 s/d	1935-9	

(a) Low frame model.

	Model	Engine position	Wheels	Seating capacity	Available	Notes
Thornycroft	A2	Front (N)	4	20 s/d	1930	
	A4	Front (N)	6	26 s/d	1930	
	A6	Front (N)	4	24 s/d	1930	
	A12	Front (N)	6	20 s/d	1930/31	
	BC	Front (N)	4	28 s/d	1930/31	
	BC	Front (F)	4	52 d/d	1930-4	(a)
	LC	Front (F)	4	52 d/d	1930/31	(a)
	XC	Front (F)	4	52 d/d	1931	
	FC	Front (F)	6	40 s/d	1930/31	
	HC	Front (F)	6	68 d/d	1930/31	
	HD trolleybus		6	56 d/d	1933	(b)
	Speedy A14	Front (N)	4	20 s/d	1931-3	
	Ardent AD	Front (N)	4	26 s/d	1931/32	
	Ardent EE	Front (N)	4	20 s/d	1934/35	
	Ardent FE	Front (F)	4	24 s/d	1934/35	
	Ardent GC	Front (N)	4	26 s/d	1935/36	
	Cygnet CD	Front (F)	4	35 s/d	1931-5	
	BD trolleybus		4	32 s/d	1933	(c)
	Daring DD	Front (F)	4	56 d/d	1931-5	
	Lightning EE	Front (N)	4	20 s/d	1934/35	
	Lightning GC	Front (N)	4	26 s/d	1935/36	
	Handy AE	Front (N)	4	20 s/d	1935/36	
	Dainty CF	Front (N)	4	24 s/d	1935-8	
	Dainty DF	Front (F)	4	24 s/d	1935-8	

	Model	Engine position	Wheels	Seating capacity	Available	Notes
	Steadfast GC	Front (N)	4	26 s/d	1935/6	
	Beautyride ZF	Front (F)	4	26 s/d	1937-9	

(a) Also available as 32-seat single-decker.
(b) Only two built (one for Nottingham, one for Derby).
(c) Only one built (as demonstrator).

	Model	Engine position	Wheels	Seating capacity	Available	Notes
TS Motors	(Tilling Stevens from 1937)					
	TS15A	Front (F)	6	68 d/d	1930/31	(a)
	TS17A	Front (F)	4	52 d/d	1930/31	(a)
	Express B9A2	Front (F)	4	32 s/d	1930	
	Express B9B2	Front (N)	4	30 s/d	1930	
	Express B10A2	Front (F)	4	32 s/d	1930/31	
	Express B10B2	Front (N)	4	30 s/d	1930-5	
	Express B10C2	Front (F)	4	40 s/d	1930/31	
	Express B39A7	Front (F)	4	32 s/d	1932-5	
	Express B39C7	Front (F)	4	40 s/d	1931/32	
	Express B49A7/B4LA7	Front (F)	4	32 s/d	1931-5	(b)
	Express B49C7	Front (F)	4	40 s/d	1931/32	
	C60A7/C6LA7	Front (F)	4	36 s/d	1932-5	(c)
	D60A6/D6LA6/D5LA6	Front (F)	4	56 d/d	1932-8	(c)(d)
	D60A7	Front (F)	4	32 s/d	1934-8	
	D60R6	Front (F)	4	56 d/d	1937/38	
	Express HA39A7	Front (F)	4	34 s/d	1935-9	
	Express H49A7/H4LA7	Front (F)	4	36 s/d	1935-9	(b)
	Express H5LA4	Front (F)	4	28 s/d	1939	(e)
	J5LA7	Front (F)	4	36 s/d	1936/37	(e)
	Successor	Underfloor	6	45 s/d	1937	(f)

(a) Petrol-electric transmission.
(b) '4L' models powered by Gardner 4LW.
(c) '6L' models powered by Gardner 6LW.
(d) '5L' models powered by Gardner 5LW.
(e) Fitted Gardner 5LW engine.
(f) Only two built (for 1937 Commercial Motor Show).

	Model	Engine position	Wheels	Seating capacity	Available	Notes
Unic (French)	M90	Front (N)	4	20 s/d	1930-2	
	M8C	Front (N)	4	28 s/d	1930-2	
	M9A	Front (N)	4	14 s/d	1932	
Vulcan	Duke	Front (N)	4	20 s/d	1930-7	
	Duchess	Front (N)	4	26 s/d	1930-7	
	Countess	Front (F)	4	28 s/d	1930	
	Prince	Front (F)	4	32 s/d	1930-6	
	Princess	Front (F)	4	36 s/d	1930	
	Emperor	Front (F)	4	51 d/d	1930-6	
Willys Overland Crossley	35 cwt	Front (N)	4	16 s/d	1930-2	
	2 ton	Front (N)	4	18 s/d	1930-2	
		Front (N)	6	20 s/d	1930-2	
W&G (W&G du Cros, London)	M	Front (N)	4	26 s/d	1930-3	
	MF	Front (F)	4	32 s/d	1930-3	
	LF	Front (F)	4	36 s/d	1930-2	
	LS	Front (N)	4	32 s/d	1930-2	

3. Bibliography

A History of London Transport, Vol 2 (T.C. Barker and M. Robbins), George Allen and Unwin, 1974.
A History of the World's Airlines (R.E.G. Davies), Oxford University Press, 1964.
Blue Triangle—AEC buses (A.A. Townsin), Transport Publishing Company, 1980.
Britain in the Nineteen Thirties (N. Branson and N. Heinemann), Weidenfeld and Nicolson, 1971.
Buses and Trolleybuses 1919 to 1945 (D. Kaye), Blandford, 1970.
Buses Annual Ian Allan, 1965 to 1982 editions.
Daimler Buses in Camera (S.J. Brown), Ian Allan, 1978.
Dennis Buses in Camera (R.N. Hannay), Ian Allan, 1980.
Dublin's Buses (P.J. Flanagan, C.B. Mac an tSaoir), Transport Research Associates, 1968.
English Journey (J.B. Priestley), Penguin, 1934.
Green Line 1930-1980 (D.W.K. Jones and B.J. Davis), London Counry, 1980.
Guy Buses in Camera (J. Pettie), Ian Allan, 1979.
History of British Bus Services, South-east England (C. Morris), Transport Publishing Company, 1980.
Looking at Buses (G.G. Hilditch), Ian Allan, 1979.
Midland Red, Vol 1 (P. Gray, M. Keeley, J. Seale), Transport Publishing Company, 1978.
Railway Motor Buses and Bus Services in the British Isles 1902-1933 (J. Cummings), Oxford Publishing Company 1978 (Vol 1), 1980 (Vol 2).
The British Motor Bus (G. Booth), Ian Allan, 1977.
The Leyland Bus (D. Jack), Transport Publishing Company, 1977.
The Man Who Built London Transport—A biography of Frank Pick (C. Barman), David and Charles, 1979.
Trolleybus (K. Blacker), Capital Transport, 1978.
Vintage Bus Annual (K. Blacker), Marshall, Harris and Baldwin, 1979.

I have also drawn upon back issues of *Buses* and *Buses Illustrated*, published monthly, the weekly *Commercial Motor* and *Motor Transport*, and upon fleet histories and other publications of the Omnibus Society and PSV Circle.

4. Acknowledgements

Unpublished material from the 1930s is, inevitably, fairly rare, and I am grateful to the many organisations and individuals who have been able to put so much my way for use in this book.

In particular, I must salute the efforts of Ron Hall of Leyland Vehicles' photographic department; Noel Jackson and Reg Westgate, custodians of the Omnibus Society's J.F. Higham collection; John Millard, manager of Victoria Coach Station; and Chris Warn, for the loan of a thesis on North-East England operators.

INDEX

Figures in italics refer to photographs